FOXES, WOLVES AND WILD DOGS OF THE WORLD

FOXES, WOLVES
AND WILD DOGS
OF THE WORLD

David Alderton

Photographs by Bruce Tanner

Facts On File

AN INFOBASE H

FOXES, WOLVES AND WILD DOGS OF THE WORLD

First published in the UK 1994
by Blandford, an imprint of Cassell plc

Facts On File, Inc.
460 Park Avenue South
New York NY 10016

Library of Congress Cataloging-in-Publication Data

David Alderton
    Foxes and wolves of the world / David Alderton.
        p.   cm.
    Includes bibliographical references and index.
    ISBN 0-8160-2954-7
    1. Foxes. 2. Wolves. I. Title.
QL737.C22P44 1994   92-46595
599.74'442—dc20   CIP

Facts On File books are available at special discounts when purchased in bulk quantities for
businesses, associations, institutions or sales promotions. Please call our Special Sales
Department in New York at 212/683-2244 or 800/322/8755.

ISBN 0-8160-2954-7

Typeset by Litho Link Limited, Welshpool, Powys, Wales
Printed and bound in China

10 9 8 7 6 5 4 3 2 1

(Previous pages) The ferocity of grey wolves (*Canis lupus*) means that they are
widely feared, but in reality, attacks on people are rare.

Contents

Acknowledgements

The photographs were taken by Bruce Tanner, except those on pages 12, 28, 101, 103, 131 (top), 132, 143, 149 (top), 162, 163, 164 (top) and 175 by the author, those on pages 119, 121 and 153 by Marian Batkiewicz, that on page 106 by US Fish and Wildlife Service and on page 116 by Steve Maslowski, US Fish and Wildlife Service.

Thanks are due to the many people who assisted in the preparation of this book, with a particular debt to the following:

Basildon Zoo, Basildon, Essex, England.
Mike Lockyer and Terry Whitaker, Port Lympne and Howletts Zoo Parks, Kent, England.
Fiesta Garden Centre, Haverhill, Suffolk, England.
Suffolk Wildlife Park, Kessingland, Suffolk, England.
Horniman Museum and Gardens, Forest Hill, London, England.
Heiner Klos, Zoo Berlin, Berlin, Germany.
Tierpark Berlin, Berlin, Germany.
Dr Jan Smielowski, Poznan Zoo, Poland.
Marian Batkiewicz, Poznan, Poland.
Dr Jim Collins, National Association of Private Animal Keepers, England.
Photographic assistants: Denise Palmer, Wendy Ashton, Bob Tanner.
Arrangements in Germany: Jeremy Tanner, Vicki Weston.

In addition, Rita Hemsley again kindly processed my handwriting on to disk, and Stuart Booth provided valuable editorial support for our endeavours.

Preface

Dogs form an integral part of the daily lives of millions of people around the world, being kept both for working purposes and increasingly, simply as companions. It is therefore ironic that the grey wolf (*Canis lupus*), as the ancestor of today's 350 or so breeds, has been pushed to the edge of extinction in Europe by hunting pressures, and is still being persecuted heavily in other parts of the world. Other species have also showed dramatic declines, such as the African wild dog (*Lycaon pictus*), whose extinction has been predicted within 20 years, unless the current population downturn can be reversed.

Tragically, it is the social species of canid that are generally under most threat today, particularly as they tend to require larger areas and tackle bigger prey. The smaller, opportunistic members of the family, such as the foxes, with their more solitary lifestyles, are the benefactors. The grey wolf (*Canis lupus*), for example, used to be the most widely distributed species of wild dog in the world, but after centuries of persecution and destruction of habitat, much of its former range in Europe has been taken over by the adaptable red fox (*Vulpes vulpes*). A similar takeover has occurred in North America, where the distribution of the coyote (*Canis latrans*) has expanded dramatically, as the wolves have declined.

With the exception of wolves, wild dogs have rarely inspired the same sense of fear and awe in people as the big cats. In a sense, they are less marketable as a result. Nevertheless, tourism can help to break down prejudice, and at the same time assist directly in the conservation of species. Already, the grey wolf is benefiting from this approach in North America and it is possible that the African hunting dog could derive a similar benefit as well.

When things do go wrong, there is now a greater chance of being able to act to conserve populations, by captive-breeding in the short-term. The encouraging start to the release scheme involving the red wolf (*Canis rufus*) in the USA shows that it is possible to reintroduce canids successfully, given favourable circumstances. Localized releases of this type may be useful for other species, such as African wild dogs, where individual populations have become isolated, assuming that a suitable environment still exists.

It is relatively easy to become complacent about the overall conservation status of wild canids, compared with other groups of mammals. The vast majority of the 34 species forming the family Canidae are not presently considered to be endangered. Indeed, no species has become extinct during the present century, and only one – the Falkland Island wolf (*Dusicyon australis*) which became extinct at the end of the last century – has disappeared over the past 400 years.

Even so, these bare figures mask the fact that seven unique subspecies of the grey wolf have been lost in just over 75 years. These include the highly distinctive Newfoundland white wolf (*Canis lupus beothucus*), a large subspecies, characterized by its white fur. The last survivor died in 1911. In Japan, the smallest form of the grey wolf, known as Shamanu (*C. l. hodophilax*) was hunted to extinction by 1905. It stood just 36 cm (14 in) high at the shoulder – smaller than many of today's breeds of domestic dog.

Such was the prejudice against wolves in North America during the early twentieth century that the state veterinary service in Montana was deliberately infecting them with sarcoptic mange, in the hope of causing an epidemic of this debilitating parasitic skin disease. Today, in more enlightened times, one of the major threats to surviving populations of wild canids is contact with domestic dogs. The spread of canine diseases into the small, surviving populations of the island grey fox (*Urocyon littoralis*) and the Simien jackal (*Canis simensis*), for example, could wipe out both species. Vaccination programmes may well be needed to safeguard the future of other wild canids as well. It would indeed be the ultimate irony if today's domestic dogs were to be directly responsible for the extinction of a wild species of canid.

David Alderton,
Brighton, England

Chapter 1
Wild Dogs and People

The feeling of primordial terror associated with the wolf is still a strong cultural instinct among the peoples of the northern hemisphere. And yet although small children may recoil in fear at the sight of wolves in the zoo, they will return home and play quite happily with a direct descendant of the grey wolf (*Canis lupus*) in the form of the domestic dog.

Throughout folklore the wolf is portrayed as a vicious and devious killer – the archetypal Big Bad Wolf in fairy stories such as *Little Red Riding Hood* and *The Three Little Pigs*. But perhaps the most frightening mythical representation is that of the werewolf – the terrifying transformation of man into wolf.

One of the earliest recorded references to the werewolf dates back to AD 125, when Marcellus Sidetes, a Roman poet, described this fearful phenomenon as an illness. According to his account, cases of this affliction were especially prevalent during the early part of the year and affected people usually retreated to cemeteries, where they eked out an existence as starving wolves.

Belief in such creatures became widespread throughout Europe and names for werewolves were incorporated into many different languages. The actual origins of this myth may come from ancient communities, where it was believed that the wearing of animal skins would reinforce a man's strength. Wherever it arose, however, by medieval times the image was firmly established throughout Europe and the search for affected individuals became something of an obsession, particularly in France. Here, over 30,000 supposedly proven cases of werewolves were documented between 1520 and 1630. Many of these unfortunate people were burnt at the stake, having first been horribly tortured. The power of the wolf exerted a tremendous effect on the human imagination.

Various rational explanations have been put forward to explain sightings of supposed werewolves. In some cases, it was probably robbers using wolf skins to terrify the local populus. In other cases, the unfortunate individual may have been suffering from lycanthropy, a psychological disorder, in which the sufferer believes that he or she is a werewolf. A number of stories refer to the use of an ointment, which helped to complete the transformation into a werewolf. It has been suggested that this could have been a hallucinogenic compound, possibly bufogenin, a substance obtained from toads. This was often used by witches to create the impression of flight, and could well have reinforced the sensation of being a werewolf.

Other cases clearly refer to people suffering from rabies. It is not uncommon for animals infected by rabies to be overtly friendly, before biting and transmitting the virus to people. The human infection can cause people to behave like mad dogs, especially in the terminal stages of the illness.

One of the most interesting explanations for lycanthropy has been put forward by Dr Lee Illis. He has proposed that an inherited condition called congenital porphyria, caused by a recessive gene, could explain at least some

While people have embraced the domestic dog (*Canis familiaris*) as a valued companion, lavishing care on their pets, they remain wary of the ancestor of all domestic dogs, the grey wolf (*Canis lupus*) (below).

cases. Sufferers from congenital porphyria develop distortions of the hands and face, and, perhaps most frighteningly, their teeth turn red. They also become very sensitive to light, which would explain a preference to go out only after dark. In the confined communities of the middle ages, the likelihood of this type of recessive trait emerging in the population would have been enhanced, and anyone displaying such symptoms undoubtedly would have aroused considerable fear in the ignorance of those times.

By the nineteenth century, public terror of werewolves had declined in the face of advances in science and medicine, but the myth was kept alive by a succession of Victorian novels and short stories. Robert Louis Stevenson, for example, explored the theme of lycanthropy in his story *Olalla*, published in 1887, a year after his famous novel *Dr Jekyll and Mr Hyde*. Perhaps the most famous novel of this genre was *The Werewolf in Paris*, written by Guy Endore, an American born in 1900, whose real name was Harry Relis.

The cinema was not slow to recognize our bizarre fascination for werewolves. The first film on the subject was a short feature called simply *The Werewolf*, made in 1913, but this was followed by various attempts of mixed merit, including Universal's 1934 production *Werewolf of London*, Lon Chaney as *The Wolf Man* in 1941 and the 1961 Hammer horror based loosely on Endore's novel, called *Curse of the Werewolf*. The 1980s saw a spate of films on the werewolf theme, including *The Howling*, *Teenwolf* and, perhaps the best in terms of quality and commercial success, Jon Landis' 1981 *An American Werewolf in London*, which managed to combine comedy, horror and some remarkable state-of-the-art special effects.

HUMAN SUCCOUR

There is another side to wolf mythology however, manifested originally by the Romans in the tale of Romulus and Remus, the legendary founders of Rome. Romulus and Remus were the illegitimate sons of the vestal virgin Rhea Silvia, and her lover, the god Mars. Legend tells how the baby twins were condemned to death and thrown into the River Tiber. However, as luck would have it, they were washed ashore in a lonely spot, where their cries attracted a female wolf. Her maternal instincts overcame her inclination to kill the helpless infants, and she suckled them, before carrying them to a cave on the Palatine Hill, overlooking Rome. In time, the children were discovered by a shepherd, and became part of his family.

This story is commemorated in the arms of the city of Rome, which incorporates the twins in its design. Incredible as it may seem, however, there do appear to be cases where wolves have actually reared children successfully. Over 50 have been documented, some dating back to the fourteenth century but others recorded in the twentieth century. One early case involved a child who had supposedly been found in the forest near Hesse, close to Hanover. A pack of wolves had adopted him when he was about 4 years old, and at the time of his capture by the local people in 1344, he showed all the behavioural characteristics of a wolf. He was naked, able only to run on all fours, and communicated by a series of grunts. He became something of a celebrity; it is known that he was even brought to England and displayed at the Court. Unfortunately, little other information is available about this early case.

More recent instances of so-called wolf-children are better documented; a number of these originate from India. There are 16 alleged cases recorded between 1843 and 1933, involving children of both sexes, who appear to have been abandoned by their parents in forested areas. One of the best-documented involved two girls, who were discovered by a Dr Singh, the rector of the orphanage at Midnapore. He first learnt of these children in October 1920, when in the Godamuri district of the country. The villagers took him to the locality where the wolves and the strange creatures could be seen.

Dr Singh told how he watched in horror and fascination as they emerged from the cave – there were three adult wolves and two younger cubs, as well as the two girls who had long hair and walked bent over on their hands and feet. He later managed to rescue the children, shooting one of the wolves in the process, only to be confronted by the confused children, who proved more dangerous and aggressive than the wolf cubs themselves.

Singh left the children with the villagers. However, when he returned later he found that they had been neglected and were in a critical condition. As a result, he then arranged for them to be taken back to his orphanage.

In all respects, the children's behaviour resembled that of wolves. They fed entirely on raw meat, and drank by lapping crouched on all fours. When opportunity presented itself, the youngsters hunted chickens around a yard,

Images of wild dogs are established in popular culture, from the time of the ancient Egyptians and their portrayals of the jackal god Anubis, up to contemporary images like this pub sign near Attlebridge in Norfolk, England.

and then raged at night when confined. If threatened, they hunched their backs like dogs, and bared their teeth.

The smaller child, christened 'Amala', died of nephritis barely a year after arriving at the orphanage. She never learnt to talk, and could only growl. Her older companion, 'Kamala' who was reckoned to be about 8 years old at the time of their capture, never integrated with human society. She was finally persuaded to drink using a glass, but continued to eat raw meat and showed an instinctive dislike of domestic dogs. Towards the end of her short and tragic life in 1929, she did learn a few words, but there was never any clue as to how she and Amala became associated with the wolf pack.

KILLER WOLVES

The grey wolves (*Canis lupus*), the largest of the Canidae, is the only species that represents a serious threat to people. Even so, attacks by wolves are far less common than popular mythology would suggest. In fact, in North America there are very few authenticated accounts of people being killed by wolves and it is now thought that the numerous stories from Eurasia of unprovoked attacks are largely exaggerated.

Nevertheless, there are always rogues, and a few individual wolves have gained notoriety for their persistent attacks on humans, and especially children. One of the most famous episodes of this type occurred in the mountainous area of Lozère, in France. It began in 1764, when a wolf struck at a woman who was looking after a herd of cattle. The wolf was actually driven away, but not before the woman was badly injured. Over that summer other attacks followed. A child was killed and partly eaten, and a further three fatal attacks occurred within weeks. The wolf became known locally as the Beast of Gevaudan, and continued its murderous habits with a vengeance.

It typically used its body weight to knock over a victim, and then ripped into the person's facial area with its teeth. Ten people were dead by November, and the army was finally called in to hunt down the wolf. They killed over 100 wolves in the area within a month, and then left, confident that one of these would have been responsible for the deaths.

But on Christmas Eve 1764, the Beast of Gevaudan struck again, with a 7-year-old boy being its next victim. A shepherd and two young girls also died in similar circumstances before the end of the year, and others followed. The wolf appeared to be becoming increasingly bold; in January it attacked a group of children and seized the youngest. The children hit back with stones, sticks and anything else they had which could be used as a weapon, and finally drove it away.

Shortly afterwards, the wolf surprised a group of three farm workers, who used their pitchforks to defend themselves, but failed to inflict a fatal blow on their attacker. The problem of tracking down the creature was immense. It could hide in the wooded, mountainous terrain, and there was no way of predicting where or when it was likely to strike again.

At this point a man with an unrivalled reputation as a wolf-hunter in France, Philippe Donneval, who had killed more than 1000 wolves in Normandy, was summoned by King Louis XV to go to Gevaudan and dispatch the beast.

Although Donneval managed to kill a number of large wolves in the region, it seems that he missed his main quarry. The attacks went on and the death toll continued to rise. A few had lucky escapes from the Beast of Gevaudan, however, such as the rider pulled from his horse close to the village of Amorgne. He managed to remount, and rode off to safety.

With Donneval's efforts proving to be in vain, the task of tracking down the wolf then passed to another of the King's confidants, Lieutenant Antoine de Bauterre, who was an experienced huntsman. He chose the best pack of hounds, assembled from those of various courtiers, and was assigned a large troop of men. Arriving in Gevaudan during late July 1765, de Bauterre was immediately confronted by further attacks and more carnage. Then, in August, the hounds discovered a huge wolf in the woods of the Abbaye Royal. After a chase and several shots, the beast was killed.

It was a cause for celebration. At last, it was thought that the Beast of Gevaudan was dead. The body was taken to Clermont Ferrand for an autopsy. In its stomach were traces of red clothing, indicating that it must have eaten human flesh. Other signs, such as its long tail – a feature described by various witnesses – appeared to confirm its identity. Then there was its size. It was the largest wolf that de Bauterre had ever seen, weighing nearly 63 kg (140 lb).

He was duly rewarded by the King and returned home, with the wolf dead and the attacks seemingly at an end. No-one was concerned at that stage, amid the celebration, that this particular wolf did not have a characteristic reddish tinge to its coat. This distinctive feature had been noted by various people who had seen or been attacked by the Beast of Gevaudan.

The attacks did not recommence until December that year, when they continued with a vengeance throughout the spring of 1766. More children died, sometimes snatched from just outside their homes. Hunting, traps and poison all failed to stem the tide of slaughter. In desperation, the local people asked the Marquis d'Apches for help, and he organized them into large-scale hunting parties. On 19 June, 300 people assembled in the Forest of la Tenaziere, including one Jean Chastel. As the beaters moved towards Chastel, a large reddish wolf broke from cover. Chastel fired, and the animal fell dead.

When this wolf was cut open, the shoulder bone of a child killed the previous day was found in its stomach. This had to be the Beast of Gevaudan, and indeed, no further attacks were recorded. Sadly, Chastel never received royal acclamation for his effort. The body of the wolf was not properly prepared for the journey to Versailles, and rotted *en route* in the summer heat. Even so, the local populace realized the debt due to him, and a public subscription saw him handsomely rewarded.

It is, of course, possible that more than one wolf was responsible for these attacks over a period of 2 years. Certainly, the fact that the wolf escaped detection for so long, while becoming increasingly bold in its attacks, suggests not only luck, but a fair degree of cunning.

The reasons as to why these attacks started is also a mystery. The wolf appeared to suffer no physical disability, which might have made it less able to catch its usual prey, as often proves to be the case with man-eating big cats. It might have been that it was simply easier to approach people on its own,

Ever watchful, the grey wolf (*Canis lupus*) makes a formidable adversary for hunters, able to move on quickly after an attack, and escape detection for long periods, as happened with the Beast of Gevaudan.

and its power meant that its hunting technique was often successful. Although there have been other cases of individual wolves attacking people, none appears to have been as deliberate and systematic as the Beast of Gevaudan.

THE ELIMINATION OF THE WOLF

As farmers gradually took over more and more land for their livestock, they came into increasing conflict with the wolf. Sheep and goats presented an easy source of prey and it is no surprise, therefore, that people sought to eliminate the wolf from their grazing lands and adjoining forests. As in Gevaudan, it was to be the wolf's domesticated relatives that were to assist in this task.

Breeds of dog developed to hunt down wolves had to combine power and speed if they were to succeed. The Irish wolfhound, standing up to 86 cm (34 in) at the shoulder, is the tallest breed of dog in the world, and was considered so valuable in seventeenth-century Britain that Oliver Cromwell forbade their export. However, once the wolf had disappeared from the British Isles, the wolfhound was no longer needed, and 50 years after the last wolf was killed in Ireland the Irish wolfhound was on the verge of extinction. Its survival today is largely due to the dedication of a Scot, Captain G.A. Graham, who managed to conserve the breed at great personal cost during the last century.

Ironically, the survival of the grey wolf in Europe today is a cause which now engenders public sympathy. Out of the 23 countries which comprise the Council of Europe, just eight still have wild wolves in their territories.

The lifestyle of the wolf is simply not compatible with modern urbanized living. The ecological niche formerly occupied by the wolf has not been left

The red fox (*Vulpes vulpes*) is now the most widely distributed canid in the world, being found throughout most of the northern hemisphere. It has also been introduced to Australia.

vacant, however; indeed, in many cities today, there are packs of feral dogs roaming the streets. The present century has also seen the rise of the urban fox. The adaptable red fox (*Vulpes vulpes*) has now taken over from the grey wolf as the most widely distributed large mammal (apart from the human race) in the northern hemisphere.

Railway embankments and similar retreats provide relatively safe earths, while scavenging ensures a reasonably plentiful food supply. Contrary to popular belief, foxes rarely take cats, although they will prey on rabbits, chickens and other similar creatures kept in suburban areas, given the opportunity.

THE FUR TRADE

A number of canids are traditionally hunted for their fur. This trade can represent a serious threat not only to a species as a whole, but also to individual populations in some areas. At least 20 of the world's 34 species of wild canid are hunted for this reason, although fur farms also exist to supply this market.

International trade in canid fur, whether from wild-caught or farmed animals, is subject to regulation under the international Convention on International Trade in Endangered Species treaty, known under its acronym of CITES. In the case of canids that are under threat of extinction, commercial trade is actually banned, with any trade only being permitted under exceptional circumstances. These species are listed on Appendix I of CITES.

The bush dog (*Speothos venaticus*) is endangered, but has not been hunted for its fur, nor heavily persecuted. The reasons for its rarity are poorly understood.

In other cases, trade may be regulated. One of the major trapping areas is North America, and here around 1½ million canids are caught annually, mainly foxes and coyotes. The available evidence suggests that this level of offtake is not proving detrimental to the wild populations. Indeed, the range of the coyote has even expanded over the past decade. A small number of grey wolves are taken in this part of the world, but their population is certainly secure here, in one of their last strongholds. Much of the trapping occurs on land that could not otherwise be used, and helps to provide an income for the indigenous peoples of the region.

Elsewhere in the world, in South America, the grey zorro (*Dusicyon griseus*) is widely trapped for its fur, with up to a million skins passing through Argentina between 1980 and 1986, most of which were destined for the then Federal Republic of Germany. This species has been traded in higher numbers than any other canid regulated by CITES.

Perhaps ironically, the two species protected from trade, to be found on Appendix I, do not play any significant part in the fur trade. These are the red wolf (*Canis rufus*) and the bush dog (*Speothos venaticus*).

At the current time, eight species of canid are included in Appendix II of CITES, effectively regulating trade in them. These include populations of the grey wolf; the grey zorro; the culpeo (*Dusicyon culpaeus*); the maned wolf (*Chrysocyon brachyurus*), the dhole (*Cuon alpinus*), Azara's zorro (*Dusicyon gymnocercus*), Blanford's fox (*Vulpes cana*) and the fennec fox (*Fennecus zerda*).

The dense fur of the Arctic fox (*Alopex lagopus*) is greatly in demand in the fur trade, with millions now being reared for this purpose on fur farms.

Even so, relatively few skins derived from these other species are traded annually, with the pelt of the maned wolf being of no commercial value.

One of the valuable functions performed by CITES is the monitoring of trade data, from both exporting and importing countries. As the number of countries becoming Parties to the Convention has increased, to the current figure of 120, so it has proved possible to build up a more complete picture of trade, and to detect any anomalies, which could be indicative of illegal trade routes. For example, trade data on the grey zorro have revealed that some of the skins come from Chile, but here, in theory at least, the species is protected and so should not be hunted.

In the case of canids, the fur trade is closely linked to demand. Fur farms have been set up in many northern countries; Scandinavia in particular has become a major centre for this activity, especially Finland. During the period 1988–89, this part of the world produced 2.6 million Arctic foxes (*Alopex lagopus*) out of a total of 3.3 million traded, with Poland accounting for a further 0.5 million specimens.

Farming has had a dramatic effect on the trapping pattern of wild Arctic foxes and other species. In North America, the numbers of Arctic foxes being trapped has fallen from about 69,000 per annum during the 1930s, down to a current figure of less than 20,000.

Conversely, the offtake of red foxes (*Vulpes vulpes*) in North America has grown considerably, more than doubling from the 1930s to the 1980s. It would appear that the actual red form is preferred over the silver variety, which tends to dominate on fur farms. Overall, about 1½ million red foxes are taken from the wild for their pelts each year.

This may partly be a reflection of the fact that red foxes are generally perceived to be a common species, and in no danger. As a result, people who may consider it socially unacceptable to wear a fur coat from any potentially threatened species will happily purchase a red fox fur coat, or a garment derived from farmed canids. While the Arctic and red foxes remain the most significant species in terms of the fur trade, raccoon dogs (*Nyctereutes procyonoides*) are also being farmed on a fairly extensive scale in Finland.

Although objections have been made against fur-farming, particularly on welfare grounds, there can be no doubting the fact that it can significantly reduce the numbers of animals taken from the wild. At present, however, the species being farmed are also among the most numerous canids in the wild, so any conservation benefit of fur-farming is negligible. Furthermore, the economic impact may mean that indigenous peoples are losing income in areas of the world where alternative employment is unlikely to be found.

CONSERVATION AND CAPTIVE BREEDING

Captive-breeding programmes are widespread in zoos and wildlife parks, both for display purposes and to assist in the conservation of endangered species. The selection pressures here clearly differ from those used in fur-farming, where the quality of the pelt and its colour, as well as the reproductive rate and ease of handling of the animals are deemed to be significant.

Breeding success in a zoo will depend on the number of animals held in captivity, their gender and age. Virtually all canids have been bred successfully in confinement over the past 30 years, although not surprisingly, the most commonly bred species tend to be those which are widely kept. Of the endangered canids, only the African wild dog (*Lycaon pictus*) breeds regularly in captivity, and during recent years, the number of litters produced in zoos has fallen from a peak during the late 1960s and early 1970s. Unfortunately, the mortality of pups bred in captivity tends to be relatively high.

This species also highlights another conservation problem which can be obscured in captive-breeding projects. While the majority of African wild dogs are of southern African stock, there has been little attempt to separate these from the eastern population, which is believed to be genetically distinct. Especially when captive-breeding is for conservation purposes, the maintenance of individual characteristics of subspecies must be respected.

Success has, however, been achieved with the red wolf (*Canis rufus*), which is the world's most endangered canid. The reintroduction scheme using captive-bred animals is already showing early signs of success, confirming that there is real hope now for its survival, at least for the foreseeable future.

Bush dogs (*Speothos venaticus*) have proved far less ready to breed in captivity, and given the vulnerable status of this species, further research to establish the difficulties involved, which may be related to its social habits, needs to be undertaken.

Few zoological collections specialize in canids, although their care is not particularly demanding, and they will often breed quite readily in such surroundings. This is a dingo (*Canis familiaris dingo*) at the Suffolk Wildlife Park, England.

A studbook has been set up to monitor stocks of the maned wolf (*Chrysocyon brachyurus*) in captivity, and prevent excessive in-breeding.

Perhaps not surprisingly, zoos have a tendency to focus their limited resources on the large or otherwise more spectacular members of a family. This can be clearly seen in the Canidae, where grey wolves (*Canis lupus*) tend to be the most popular exhibit. In contrast, the grey zorro (*Dusicyon griseus*), whose skins are extensively traded, is a rarity in zoos, along with many of the other smaller foxes. In fairness, this species is not considered to be at risk, but the knowledge about its biology that could be obtained by captive-breeding would give great insight into this heavily exploited member of the Canidae.

One of the problems in the past with breeding rare canids in zoological collections is that stock may be scattered around the world. The logistics, not to mention the expense, of moving animals for breeding purposes often proved a barrier.

Technology is helping to break down these barriers. The use of DNA testing can contribute greatly to breeding programmes, indicating the most suitable pairings to avoid the potentially deleterious effects of in-breeding, in the case of small zoo populations. Studbooks are now established for various species, in which this and other relevant information can be recorded. The African wild dog (*Lycaon pictus*), the bush dog (*Speothos venaticus*) and the maned wolf (*Chrysocyon brachyurus*) are three species for which studbook schemes exist.

Artificial insemination is also now feasible, so that it is no longer necesssary to move an animal to another country for breeding purposes. Similarly, embryo transplants can be used, following *in vitro* fertilization, if required. The use of such techniques greatly enhances the possibilities of success within breeding programmes.

Unlike many groups of larger carnivore, the Canidae in general are not currently under great threat of extinction. This may in part be a reflection of the opportunistic and adaptable nature of many species. Where there is a serious problem, however, as in the case of the red wolf, most zoologists would agree that a breeding programme must be established in the country of the species' origin, so as to facilitate release projects at a future date. Clearly, however, it is also vital to address the cause of the species' decline, if there is to be any hope of returning it successfully to its native habitat.

Conflict with local people is a major reason for the persecution of canids. Ever since the first flocks of sheep, goats and cattle grazed under a herdsman's watchful eye, so wolves, for example, have been targeted as a potential threat. At least 21 out of the 34 species of canid will attack domestic stock, and this can have critical conservation implications. For example, the threat posed by species such as the endangered Simien jackal (*Canis simensis*) is often seriously exaggerated.

Detailed studies of the effects of predation by canids have been carried out in North America involving the coyote (*Canis latrans*) and grey wolf (*Canis lupus*). The average loss varies, even in areas where wild canids are relatively numerous. In the western part of the USA, young lambs are probably most vulnerable to coyotes, with losses between 4 and 8 per cent being recorded. One of the major difficulties, however, in any such assessment is how to determine the exact cause of mortality. It may be that the animal in question had already died, and that the coyotes were simply scavenging. The fact that a canid is observed feeding on a carcass is not definite proof that it was in any way responsible for the animal's death.

The situation becomes even more complex when compensation is paid by government bodies for livestock losses resulting from attacks by wild canids.

Grey wolves (*Canis lupus*) have resorted to scavenging in some parts of Europe. Attacks on farmstock are often falsely attributed to wolves. They are more likely to be caused by packs of feral dogs in some areas.

Investigations into alleged cases of predation by wolves on cattle in Minnesota revealed that over 70 per cent of the carcasses involved had apparently disappeared. Furthermore not all of the calves reported missing as the result of attacks by wolves may even have existed! This is because ranchers sometimes turn out cattle which they believe to be pregnant, and then ascribe the loss of calves to wolves if the individual cows are not subsequently seen to have calves with them. In over a quarter of cases, according to one investigation, the cows were not actually pregnant in the first place!

It is also clear that not only wolves may attack farmstock in this area of the USA, and yet they invariably are deemed to be the culprits. In 10 per cent of cases, closer investigations revealed that coyotes were responsible. In other parts of the world, feral domestic dogs rather than coyotes may kill sheep, and yet it is always the wolf that is held responsible. Reports from both Italy and Spain confirm that in over half the cases investigated, wolves were blameless.

In most areas, livestock losses to wild canid predators are below 2 per cent, even in regions where they are numerous. It is clear that young animals are more likely to fall victim than older stock, with sheep and goats being favoured over cattle, which represent a larger and more difficult target.

The habitat may also influence the level of predation on domestic stock. Cattle grazing in areas where there is tall growth are twice as likely to fall victim to wolves, compared with those kept on open pastures, according to one study carried out in Alberta. By choosing grazing pasture carefully, therefore, it should be possible to reduce the incidence of attacks.

There is also some evidence to suggest that wolves prefer to depend on their natural quarry, rather than attacking farmstock, at least in some parts of their range. Observations from Minnesota in a severe winter reveal that white-tailed deer fawns (*Odocoileus virginianus*) are more susceptible to wolf attack and this correlates with a reduction in the numbers of domestic animals lost.

Concern over fox predation on game birds has long been a concern of land holders, but recent studies suggest that attempts to control the numbers of foxes are not necessarily cost-effective. Red foxes (*Vulpes vulpes*) do not occur at high population densities, and the effect of killing is simply likely to draw others into the area to fill the vacated niche.

Where there has been an attempt to eliminate foxes from an area entirely, then usually a slight increase in the numbers of chicks can be seen, but this is not maintained in the adult population. Other factors, such as the land use pattern may well have a more significant bearing by this stage. The level of other prey, notably the availability of small mammals, also affects the extent of predation experienced by the game bird population. When these are plentiful, less game birds are likely to fall victim to foxes.

Under normal circumstances, foxes will only kill sufficient for their needs, but should they gain access to a confined pen of birds, then they are likely to slaughter more than they require. This is not a blood lust, but rather a response to the mass panic in the birds, disturbed by a predator and unable to escape their confinement.

It used to be thought that it would be possible to use the killing instincts of predators such as the red fox to curb populations of other animals, in particular, rabbits. This was certainly the hope in Australia, although originally, foxes had been taken there simply for hunting purposes. The initial

Red foxes (*Vulpes vulpes*) playing together on a farm. Today, their numbers are probably higher than at any time in the past.

release of foxes brought from England occurred close to Melbourne, Victoria, in 1845, but it was not until the 1870s that the first successful releases took place. In practice, it was found that although the foxes survived, they did not have any significant effect on the rabbit population overall. Luckily, they do not appear to have had a severe impact on Australia's native fauna either; it seems that they prefer to feed on dead sheep, as well as poultry and rabbits.

Another direct attempt to control introduced rabbits by means of a canid predator was carried out much more recently, in the late 1940s, on Tierra del Fuego at the tip of South America. In the light of the Australian experience, this attempt was almost doomed to failure from the outset, especially since the native canid, the culpeo (*Dusicyon culpaeus*), had failed to exert any control on the rabbit population. When 24 grey zorros (*Dusicyon griseus*) were released here, the number of rabbits was already estimated to be over 30 million. The culpeo itself would have been a better option, had it not been heavily persecuted, as about 20 per cent of its diet is naturally comprised of rabbits. By way of contrast, rabbits make up only 3 per cent of the grey zorro's normal prey.

Instead of curbing the numbers of rabbits, the grey zorros turned to the ruddy-headed geese (*Chloephaga rubidiceps*) for food, and caused a decline in their numbers. Then the spread of the myxomatosis virus caused the rabbit population to crash, and all the foxes were forced to adapt their feeding habits accordingly.

The cost of protecting stock from wild dogs can be high, and in many cases, it may not be justified by the scale of the losses. Various methods can be used, depending on the individual situation, and, increasingly, public opinion.

Killing grey wolves (*Canis lupus*) in an area is simply likely to trigger an increase in the reproductive rate of the population in that region. They can be prolific.

Hunting is a long-standing method of control of the red fox, although there are arguments about its efficacy. Vocal campaigns by pressure groups calling for a ban on hunting in Britain have already meant that tracts of the country-side here have become inaccessible to hunts and killing foxes in adjacent areas simply means that others will move in to occupy this vacant territory.

Foxes are potentially very prolific, as shown by the populations now found in urban areas, and a dramatic reduction in their numbers would be necessary to curb their spread. Since the red fox is the major carrier of rabies in mainland Europe (see page 28), this is a critical argument. Here is an animal that represents not only a threat to livestock, but the human population as well. It may be for this reason that anti-hunting groups appear to receive less support in parts of Europe where rabies is endemic, as in France.

Any regulation of wolf numbers in North America would also demand a considerable slaughter. Nature adapts, and when populations are low in a given area, so more females in a pack will breed. As the wolf population is reduced, so its reproductive rate is likely to rise. In fact, research has shown that it may well be necessary to cull more than half the population in a given area annually, to have any depressive effect on the numbers of wolves.

While traditional methods of killing canids, such as steel leghold traps and poisons, are increasingly unacceptable on welfare and environmental grounds, the costs of hunting can become prohibitive in financial terms. In Iceland, for example, where up to 4 per cent of the island's lambs are killed each year by Arctic foxes (*Alopex lagopus*), the government spends about US$200,000 on a control programme, using professional hunters. They kill on average 900 out of an estimated adult population of 2000 Arctic foxes here, as well as around 1300 cubs annually, working throughout the year. In spite of this intense persecution, however, the loss of sheep continues, and may cost the farmers up to US$3.6 million. There is also clear evidence that in spite of nearly 50 per cent of the adult population of foxes being killed each year, their numbers are continuing to rise, at least in some areas of the island.

There may be other methods that can help to reduce the conflict between wild canids and farmers. Perhaps not surprisingly, one of the best means of deterring attacks is to use dogs as flock guards in among the herds of sheep. This was the system used in Europe, as a means of guarding against wolf attacks, when they were widespread.

Particular breeds of dog, some of which still survive today, were developed specifically as flock guardians, ready to defend the flock against attack. Many, such as the Maremma sheepdog from Italy, or the kuvasz and komondor, which originated in the region of present-day Hungary, were creamish-white in colour, enabling them to blend in among the sheep. All are powerfully built dogs, typically weighing over 50 kg (110 lb), and worked alongside smaller breeds, kept for herding purposes.

Recent investigations have suggested that the use of such dogs and the presence of shepherds are the most effective means of deterring attacks on sheep by both coyotes and wolves. Close supervision of the flock is also important, so that sick or dying individuals can be segregated, and at lambing

The Arctic fox (*Alopex lagopus*) is heavily hunted in Iceland, with nearly half the entire population being killed here by hunters each year, but population growth is still continuing in some areas of the island.

time, no carrion should be left in the pastures. This can serve to attract wild canids, which may in turn progress to attacking the sheep themselves.

Other methods, such as the use of baits containing chemicals which depress fertility may be more widely used in the future. In a recent survey in the USA this ranked higher in terms of public acceptance than killing offending animals, but it could cause wider concern in the longer term. A simpler option may be to encourage farmers to change from sheep or goats to cattle in areas where coyotes are prevalent.

CANIDS AND DISEASE
The close association between carnivore and prey can also have further far-reaching economic and social consequences, in terms of the spread of disease. The introduction of the red fox to Australia (see page 23), for example, also brought *Echinococcus* tapeworms. These internal parasites have a two stage life-cycle, typically relying on herbivores such as sheep or cattle as intermediate hosts.

The adult tapeworms, which in this instance are relatively small, usually only measuring 5 mm (¼ in) in length, produce eggs which are voided in the fox's faeces. These then contaminate grazing pasture, being washed out of the spoor, and are likely to be ingested by grazing herbivores. The life-cycle is completed when the immature tapeworm in the body of the herbivore is consumed by a carnivore. Within the herbivore, the young tapeworm encysts, usually in the lungs and liver. *Echinococcus* is a particular danger because it can spread to humans, who act as an intermediate host, and this may give rise to brain cysts, which can be fatal.

Domestic dogs are likely hosts as well. This is why they should not be fed on raw offal or other meat, and must be dewormed regularly. Suitable treatment is available to kill the adult tapeworms, and a dog can have several thousands in its intestinal tract, without any obvious symptoms.

A number of different tapeworms have been identified in different parts of the world, with *Echinococcus vogeli*, for example, being recorded in South America, affecting both the domestic dog and the bush dog (*Speothos venaticus*), which appears to be the natural host. This tapeworm cycles through rodents, using the pacas (*Cuniculus* spp.) and other similar species as its intermediate host.

In recent years, another *Echinococcus* tapeworm, *E. multilocularis*, has spread southwards from the Arctic area of North America, and has been found in western parts of both Canada and the USA. Wolves and possibly coyotes may be implicated in its spread; it is rarely encountered in domestic dogs.

These tapeworm infections have an economic cost, because apart from the costs of prophylactic treatment, any affected carcasses of sheep and other herbivores will be condemned in the slaughterhouse. Tapeworm infections have had serious effects on Australia's meat exports, and it is hard to eliminate them when wild canids and domestic herbivores are in close proximity to each other.

The most serious disease transmissible to people from wild canids is, however, the viral infection rabies. Although a number of other mammals can spread this disease, the Canidae represent the greatest risk worldwide.

Greatest concern has been focused in Europe on the red fox (*Vulpes vulpes*), but other species can represent an equivalent threat in other parts of the world, ranging from the Arctic fox (*Alopex lagopus*) in the far north to black-backed jackals (*Canis mesomelas*) in southern Africa.

The virus is present in the saliva of an infected animal, and is usually spread by a bite, although an open cut can be equally hazardous. There are many different strains of the virus, which may be 'host-adapted'. Foxes, for example, are most vulnerable to the viral strain which predominates in Europe.

In the past, efforts to control the spread of rabies in the fox population focused on the need to reduce the contact rate between an infected individual and others in the area. If the healthy foxes could be killed, then there would be less risk of the infection surviving in the population. Aspects of fox biology influence the likelihood of transmission as well, however, with cubs capable of spreading the disease as they travel in search of their own territory. In most cases, foxes do not suffer from the furious form of rabies which often strikes dogs, and so they do not rampage over a wide area in the terminal stages of the disease.

The current spread of rabies across Europe began during World War 2, and has now progressed about 1500 km (900 miles) westwards. Its annual advance is about 60 km (36 miles) on average, although eruptions can see the disease move forward at a faster rate.

Mortality is high when the infection enters a susceptible population for the first time, and many of the foxes die, leaving the disease quiescent. Subsequently, as new foxes move into the territory, secondary waves of infection are probable, especially in the late winter, when such movements are most common.

The infection usually spreads between foxes as a result of fighting. In the new host the virus multiplies and then travels via the peripheral nervous system into the central nervous system and finally to the brain. The incubation period is variable, and typically related to the location of the bite relative to the brain. It can vary from about 15 days to 7 weeks or more.

The risk to people can be either direct, via the bite of a rabid fox, or through contact with a domestic dog that has been attacked by a rabid fox. On occasions, especially where wolves are involved, farmstock such as cattle may be infected, with larger animals often becoming unmanageable and even vicious in the terminal stages of the disease.

In a bid to control rabies, domestic animals in endemic areas may be vaccinated, while thousands of foxes have been killed each year in Europe, in an attempt to control the spread of the disease. Shooting, and gassing the foxes in their dens are the favoured methods for this purpose.

Overall, however, these attempts have been a failure. Only in Denmark has there been a notable success. Here, on three occasions the disease has been eliminated in just 2 years through the use of gassing and poisoned baits.

In other parts of the world, massive slaughter of all animals in infected areas has been carried out, with little obvious success. In Alberta, Canada, there was an attempt to overcome the disease in 1953 by a ruthless eradication campaign. It left 50,000 red foxes, 35,000 coyotes and 4200 wolves dead, as well as a host of other species, including various wild cats, bears and skunks.

A different approach to controlling rabies began during 1978. Attempts to use a vaccine to protect foxes against rabies commenced in Switzerland, using the natural topography of the landscape to assist in these trials. At one entrance to a valley, as many foxes as possible were killed, while at the other entry point, chicken heads doused with oral vaccine were left out for the foxes to eat, and gain immunity as a result.

Follow-up studies revealed that although foxes with rabies had moved into the area where the original population was largely wiped out, the virus had not been able to spread into the region where the vaccine had been used. There were concerns, however, that the vaccine represented a hazard to other species, as it was manufactured from live rabies virus, whose pathogenicity had been reduced; a so-called live, attenuated viral vaccine.

Nevertheless, this programme proved an overwhelming success. Over 600,000 doses of the vaccine, called SAD ERA, were used through 45,000 km^2 (17,400 square miles) of the country. Rabies was almost entirely eliminated from Switzerland by 1985, just 7 years after vaccination had begun.

Other countries have adopted similar systems, and safer vaccines are now in use. Genetic engineering has helped in this regard. The *Vaccinia* virus, which helped to eliminate smallpox, has been modified, with critical parts of the rabies vaccine being introduced into it. These are sufficient to evoke an immune response in foxes given this modified vaccine.

Further trials are being carried out in other European countries where rabies is endemic. At present the infection is widespread throughout the world, being generally absent only from islands such as the British Isles and Australia. Current results with the vaccine programme suggest it may only be a matter of time before the incidence of the disease is dramatically reduced. In Germany, for example, rabies has virtually been eliminated from the south, where an eradication programme was undertaken using baits containing a vaccine. Over 5 million of these were used between 1983 and 1987, and tests have shown that about three-quarters of the foxes subsequently shot in these areas had gained immunity to the disease.

The use of oral vaccines has proved to be a major breakthrough in the battle against rabies. It is both cheaper and more effective than attempts to kill off the foxes, and is also less socially disruptive: an important consideration when the movement of foxes plays a key part in the spread of the infection.

Elsewhere in the world, vaccination programmes of this type could prove to be a vital conservation tool, protecting endangered canids from outbreaks of this disease. In Europe itself, scientists are cautiously optimistic that rabies may almost be eliminated from the continent by the end of the millennium.

Chapter 2
Form and Function

Unlike many other carnivores, dogs spend most of their time on the ground, and are ideally suited to a terrestrial lifestyle. They are adaptable by nature, however, and this generalization is reflected in their anatomy. Wild dogs occur in a wide range of habitats, from the frozen wastelands of the far north to the searing deserts of the Middle East, and not surprisingly, members of the family show various adaptations that enable them to thrive under different environmental conditions.

In size, canids range from the fennec fox (*Fennecus zerda*), weighing around 1.5 kg (3 lb) up to the northern grey wolf (*Canis lupus*), which can weigh 80 kg (176 lb).

HEAD AND SKULL

Most canids have 42 teeth, all of which are paired, except for the molars, of which there are two in each side of the upper jaw, with three below.

At the front of the mouth, the incisors are relatively large and slightly curved. These are used to seize hold of prey, and tear at the carcass, in conjunction with the canines, located behind them. The canines themselves are bigger and pointed, and play an important part in overcoming struggling prey. In contrast to those of some other carnivores, such as cats, however, the canines are not especially sharp. The lower canines are positioned so that they fit just in front of the corresponding teeth in the upper jaw, with a small gap, known as a diastema, separating the canines from the premolars. The diastema allows the canines to lock together when the mouth is shut.

The premolars are the most numerous group of teeth, with four in each jaw. The last premolars in the upper jaw are modified, as in other members of the Carnivora, to operate in conjunction with the first lower molar teeth, as carnassial teeth. Their combined action serves to cut through flesh with a scissor-like mechanism. The peaks, called cusps, are flattened at the rear of the premolar, and the front of the molar, and are not positioned in straight lines, but arranged in the shape of an open 'V'. This helps to prevent the item of food slipping forward in the mouth. Even so, dogs adopt a fairly characteristic pose when chewing with their carnassial teeth, holding their head tilted downwards on one side.

The upper premolar forming part of the carnassial arrangement is considerably larger than the other premolars, which are also less specialized in terms of their structure. Each premolar in the lower jaw, as with the canines, is located in front of its corresponding number in the upper jaw. The central cusps of the premolars therefore fit between the opposing gaps in the other jaw.

This explains the presence of three molars in the lower jaw, compared with just two in the upper jaw. The first molar in the lower jaw forms part of the

Canids seize food with their incisors, with their pointed canines penetrating into the flesh, as shown by this bush dog (*Speothos venaticus*). The lower canine is clearly highlighted in the photograph.

The carnassial teeth are used to break up the prey, so that it can be swallowed. Canids typically use their carnassial teeth with their head leaning towards one side, as shown here by this fennec fox (*Fennecus zerda*).

carnassial system, and also corresponds with the first molar in the upper jaw, towards its rear. The molar teeth are used for crushing and macerating food so that it can be swallowed. Dogs tend not to spend long actually chewing, unless they have a bone or are eating nuts of some sort for example. They generally bolt their food in chunks rather than small pieces. This enables them to consume relatively large amounts in a short period of time, before they are driven off their kill by other, larger carnivores such as hyaenas.

Dietary modifications of the teeth can be seen in some species, such as the raccoon dog (*Nyctereutes procyonoides*), whose food intake is based on vegetables, fruit and insects rather than large prey. Here the molars are relatively large for grinding purposes, and there may well even be an extra molar present in the upper jaw, giving a total of 44 teeth. With less tearing of flesh necessary, the carnassial teeth of the raccoon dogs are underdeveloped with a small cutting area.

Further specialization is evident in the bat-eared fox (*Otocyon megalotis*), which is mainly insectivorous. The hard chitinous casing of many insects is relatively indigestible, and so the grinding action of the molars is important. The bat-eared fox has therefore evolved with three or four upper molars, and as many as five in the lower jaw, giving it more teeth than any other canid, varying from 46 to 50 depending on the individual. The carnassial shearing system is also not evident in this species, although there are other anatomical adaptations related to its diet evident in the structure of the jaw and musculature (see pages 33–4).

In most canids, there is a fundamental dichotomy between the functioning of the canines, and that of the carnassial teeth located further back in the mouth. In order to be effective, the jaws need to be opened wide to provide the

The positioning of the teeth in the lower jaw, in front of their counterparts in the upper jaw, can be seen here. The sagittal crest is also evident, as the raised area at the back of this grey wolf (*Canis lupus*) skull, and is an important area for muscle attachments.

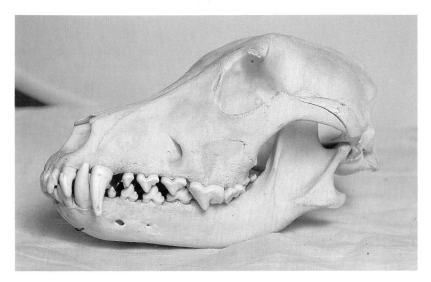

necessary force to enable the canine teeth to be driven home into the canid's prey. No lateral movement is required in this instance whereas it is, of course, essential for the functioning of the carnassial teeth, so they are properly positioned with regard to each other. In addition, a sideways action also assists the efficiency of the molar teeth in grinding up food.

Two muscle masses serve to close the jaws with complementary actions: the masseter and the temporalis muscle. The masseter attaches just beneath the eye socket on the upper part of the skull and asserts its greatest influence when the jaws are almost closed. The temporalis muscle originates from a higher position on the skull than the masseter, arising from the lateral surface of the brain case and the area behind the eye. Its fibres insert on the highest point of the lower jaw – the coronoid process – and so are directed both vertically and backwards as well, in the case of the posterior part of this muscle mass.

The anterior muscle fibres of the temporalis attached to the coronoid are well-placed to initiate the closing of the jaws; this action then shifts posteriorly through this muscle mass to the masseter as the angle of the jaw is reduced.

The positioning of the jaws relative to each other is controlled by various other muscle groups. Pterygoideus and the superficial masseter, for example, enable the jaws to be moved forwards, while others allow for backward, lateral and medial movements. This means that slight adjustments can be made in response to almost any situation, to enable the carnassial teeth to function effectively, irrespective of whether meat itself or a bone is being gnawed.

In addition to the jaws, of course, the dog may also use its forefeet to hold down part of a carcass and make it easier to dismember portions with its jaws. When it comes to opening the jaws, this is simply carried out by the digastric muscle, which attaches at the rear of the skull and on the lower edge of the mandible.

Note the contraction of skull length evident in this bulldog skull, compared with that of the wolf. It has become more rounded in shape.

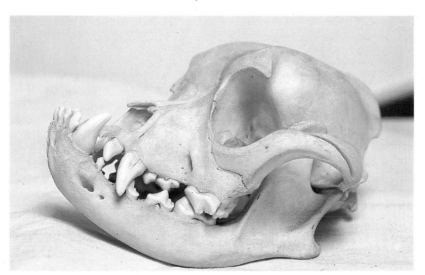

The snout of this grey fox (*Urocyon cinereoargenteus*) is relatively narrow, indicating that it tends to prey on small mammals and invertebrates, rather than larger prey. In contrast, the African wild dog (*Lycaon pictus*), preying on larger herbivores, has a correspondingly broader muzzle to seize its prey effectively.

At this point on the jaw of the bat-eared fox (*Otocyon megalotis*) there is a flange of bone – the subangular lobe. This is absent in all other species apart from the raccoon dog (*Nyctereutes procyonoides*), in which it is smaller, and its presence is almost certainly related to diet. Both of these species prey upon invertebrates – the bat-eared fox in particular being highly insectivorous – and the subangular lobe, by altering the point of insertion of the digastric muscle which attaches to it, greatly improves the efficiency of the jaw opening process. This is clearly a vital attribute when catching small and relatively nimble invertebrates.

In contrast, the power of the canines is largely redundant when catching small prey. This is reflected by the less powerful jaw muscles, and corresponding skeletal changes. The top of the skull is smooth, with no raised attachment area, known as the sagittal crest, towards the rear, and the temporalis muscles are reduced in size. The zygomatic arch is also relatively slender in such species.

Overall, since these canids do not have to seize large prey, their snouts have become relatively slender. This enables them to poke around between rocks and under bushes to catch invertebrates and other small creatures.

THE CANID SKELETON

The skeletal structure of all members of the Canidae is remarkably consistent. This is largely a reflection of a lack of specialization in terms of lifestyle. Canids can run, dig and even swim. The most notable feature of their skeleton, when compared with that of other carnivores, is the length of the limbs relative to the body size. Most canids, with the notable exception of the short-legged raccoon dog (*Nyctereutes procyonoides*) stand quite tall.

Like all other carnivores, the Canidae have seven cervical vertebrae. These are bound together with strong muscle attachments, giving the powerful neck used to pull down prey while running. The number of thoracic vertebrae supporting the ribs is also relatively consistent, numbering 13 or 14 in total. The ribs themselves may be quite long, creating a deep chest to accommodate the lungs and heart. This is a typical feature associated also with domestic breeds of dog which run at speed, such as greyhounds.

The sternum, or breastbone, to which the ribs attach at the base of the chest, is not completely ossified, and this enables the chest to move as the animal breathes. The last pair of ribs are described as 'floating', because they do not attach to the sternum.

The powerful lumbar region is made up of 6–8 vertebrae, with 3 or 4 comprising the sacral area, attaching to the pelvis. The greatest variance in the vertebral column occurs in the tail area. Most canids, especially those which pursue their prey, such as wolves, have a relatively long tail. This helps with balance when they are running and turning at speed. The tail is also important for communication purposes, especially in the case of species such as the African wild dog (*Lycaon pictus*), which hunt in a group, and may end in a conspicuous white tip. Some species, such as the raccoon dog (*Nyctereutes procyonoides*), have a very short tail compared with the length of their body. The number of caudal vertebrae comprising the tail can therefore vary from 14 to 23 in total.

The rigid structure of the canid vertebral column restricts dogs to either a trotting or galloping mode. They are not able to bound along like cats, the more developed dorsal spines restricting flexibility of the column.

In the case of the limb bones, the scapula (shoulder blade) at the top of the front limb has become flattened and rectangular in shape, while the clavicle (collar bone) has virtually disappeared. The shape of the scapula means that it can contribute to the stride length, enabling the canid to cover more ground in a single stride. In contrast, the clavicle would only serve to slow down the animal, since it would pull the shoulder in a lateral direction, thus reducing the available propulsive thrust.

The limb bones themselves are also elongated, contributing to the length of stride, while lower down, the feet are adapted to withstand the shock of impact as the canid runs. The fact that dogs walk on their toes (digitigrade) also makes a small contribution to stride length, enabling a dog to cover more ground in a single movement.

Even so, long legs may not be linked entirely to speed. The maned wolf (*Chrysocyon brachyurus*) has particularly long legs, but is not especially swift. It is believed that their height enables them to have good visibility in the grassland areas of South America where they are found.

Another feature of the maned wolf is the partial fusion of the central supporting pads on the underside of the foot. These pads help to cushion the foot as it impacts with the ground. Although appearing to be hard, they are, in fact, highly vascularized and a deep cut here can result in a considerable loss of blood.

35

The maned wolf (*Chrysocyon brachyurus*) is actually more closely allied to foxes, in spite of its name, and uses its height to give it visibility.

Dogs are generally able to run and jump, and even swim as shown here by this dingo (*Canis familiaris dingo*), but they rarely climb, with the exception of the grey fox (*Urocyon cinereoargenteus*) which has agile front legs.

The lower parts of all the limbs are strengthened with strong attachments of ligaments, and the wrist is stabilized, as is the ankle, to restrict lateral movement. In all dogs, a reduction in the number of digits in contact with the ground is apparent. The innermost digit on the forelimb – equivalent to the human thumb – is still present, but is higher up the leg, forming the so-called 'dew claw', in all species but the African wild dog. Hind dew claws are usually only found on domestic dogs, rather than their wild relatives, who normally possess only four toes here.

Reduction in the length of the metacarpal bones underlies the positioning of the dew claw. In this position, it will not come into contact with the ground, but may still be useful to the dog for striking out at prey. It is sharp, and capable of inflicting a nasty injury. The forelegs are not only used for locomotion, they are also used to restrain quarry, and there would be little purpose in having dew claws present on the hindlimbs for catching prey.

The claws of canids are not retractable, and as a consequence, they tend to be blunt, because they are in almost permanent contact with the ground. They are relatively broad in shape, and help to give a grip, especially when the dog is running.

In the majority of canids, the tibia and fibula bones in the hindlimbs are bound together in the vicinity of the ankle (hock) joint. The knee joint above is more flexible, but the overall effect is to reduce lateral movement. This is particularly important in the case of the hindlimbs, which provide the thrust for locomotion, although a similar situation is evident in the forelimbs of most species as well, with the radius and ulna held together to prevent rotation. The notable exception to this is the grey fox (*Urocyon cinereoargenteus*), however, which frequently climbs trees. Rigidity of the forelimbs would make climbing

37

both difficult and dangerous, so the grey fox has evolved greater freedom for its limbs to rotate, enabling it to maintain and adjust its balance easily, as it climbs among the branches.

In canids as a group, there is less specialization apparent in limb structure than that seen in herbivores. The humerus and radius in the forelimb, for example, are of roughly equal length, and the musculature remains quite evenly distributed down the entire limb. Herbivores, in contrast, have a significantly shorter humerus, relative to the radius, with the musculature here tending to be concentrated at the top part of the limb. This lightens the lower part, enabling the animal to run with correspondingly less effort. This lack of specialization probably reflects the need for dogs to swim, dig and hold their prey as well as run.

COAT

In terms of colour, there is a remarkable consistency within the Canidae. All species, with the notable exception of the African wild dog (*Lycaon pictus*), are generally uniform in coloration, with markings usually confined to the head and tip of the tail. African wild dogs have a very individual pattern of markings, with black blotches breaking up the paler areas of fur, which may help individuals to recognize each other from a distance. In many species, the hair on the abdomen is lighter than elsewhere on the body.

There may be considerable variance in coloration through the range of a species, however. For example, the nominate race of grey wolf, *C.l. lupus*, found in the forests of Asia and Europe, has relatively dark fur, whereas tundra wolves (*C.l. albus*) found further north have a much paler coat. This variation helps the wolves to conceal their presence more effectively in their own particular natural environment.

A more sophisticated version of colour modification for the purpose of camouflage is seen in the case of the Arctic fox (*Alopex lagopus*), which turns white or pale blue in winter to conceal its presence against a snowy background. There are other problems to be faced however, aside from the changing Arctic landscape. The temperature range in this region is more variable through the year than in most temperate areas, fluctuating from as low as −60°C (−76°F) up to 20°C (68°F) in the summer. Arctic foxes have a winter coat which provides them with unrivalled insulation in the winter, but at the start of the spring, the dense underfur is shed, leaving essentially just the guard hairs, which offer far less insulation. When autumn comes, the undercoat grows again, and the guard hairs become longer.

Temperature appears to have no effect on the change in coloration of the coat; Arctic foxes kept in temperate areas still show the characteristic white fur during the winter months. In the case of the blue form of this species, it simply becomes paler, rather than white.

It appears that species which are naturally found in temperate parts of the world may have a slightly different moulting pattern. The cycle is more protracted and less defined, starting in the spring, and continuing through to the autumn, with the underfur growing back slowly from the late summer onwards.

Colour variants in species other than the Arctic fox are not unknown in the

African wild dogs (*Lycaon pictus*) have a highly individual patterning.

Canidae, but they tend to be uncommon. A study based on nearly 3000 skins of the red fox (*Vulpes vulpes*) in Finland, revealed that 99 per cent were of the normal reddish phase. The remaining 1 per cent consisted of black-bellied individuals (0.6 per cent), pure black foxes (0.1 per cent) and so-called 'cross' foxes (0.3 per cent), with a distinctive band of darker hair traversing the shoulders, and running down the back towards the tail, creating the appearance of a cross. This feature may be evident in ordinary foxes, but it is particularly emphasized in these cross foxes.

Other colour variants of the red fox have been recorded in different parts of its range. Occasional albinos have been documented in Britain, both from Whaddon Chase, and Dartmoor; these are whitish in coloration, with distinctive pink eyes. Melanistic foxes, which are blackish in colour, may in fact be more common in Finland and other northern areas than elsewhere. They are nevertheless rare. In England, there is a record of a black fox being killed by the Belvoir Hunt, back in 1850, and the most recent report relates to a black fox which has been seen and photographed roaming in the vicinity of Turners Hill, near Crawley in East Sussex, during the early part of 1993.

As with wolves, there appears to be a variation in the coloration of red foxes depending upon their environment. Those in upland areas tend to have a brighter coat than foxes ranging closer to sea level, with the former being of a bright, golden-red shade whereas the latter may be of a paler, yellower tone.

The coloration of a fox remains the same throughout its life, although it may become slightly paler in adult animals during the summer months. Cubs

Grey wolves (*Canis lupus*) may vary considerably in colour through their range, as shown by these two individuals.

born in the winter have a thick coat which gives them good insulation. Then, during the spring, the longer guard hairs start to emerge. It will be a further year before they start to moult fully for the first time.

Light exposure does affect the moulting cycle. If foxes are given conditions of increased daylength before they have started to moult in the spring, this does not initiate an early moult. However, an increased photoperiod introduced later on will serve to speed up the moult by about a month.

It is no coincidence that the facial area, as well as the tail may be coloured differently in canids. These are the parts of the body used for communication purposes, and a variance in coloration here will emphasize facial or tail movements.

Some of the hairs on the snout have become specialized for sensory purposes. These whiskers, or vibrissae, occur around the facial area arranged in tufts. Those along the side of the snout are most highly developed, and prominent. The intra-ramal tuft on the underside of the lower jaw appears to be more significant in some species than others however, and this may be related to the lifestyle of the canid concerned. Most canids will sniff the ground on occasions, and this is when these vibrissae are most likely to be employed. It is no coincidence that in the short-legged bush dog (*Speothos venaticus*) these whiskers are relatively well-developed, in contrast to the maned wolf (*Chrysocyon brachyurus*), for example, which inhabits less open ground.

Fighting is not unknown in packs of wild dogs, and this dhole (*Cuon alpinus*) bears the scars of such an encounter on its ears.

The bush dog (*Speothos venaticus*) is well-equipped with sensory whiskers, as shown here, on the sides of the face and above the eyes.

Adaptations to individual environments can be seen in some species with regard to the presence of hair on the feet, although this may be for different reasons. Both the fennec fox (*Fennecus zerda*) and Tibetan fox (*Vulpes ferrilata*), for example, have their pads well-covered with hair, but to protect them from scorching desert sand and snow respectively.

THE SENSES

Canids rely largely on a combination of hearing and eyesight to track their prey, with the relative significance of each sense depending on the individual species and their lifestyle. Many wild dogs are partially nocturnal as well, causing a shift in their sensory requirements. Smell is also important, confirming the relatively non-specialist nature of this family.

It is interesting that the size of the ear flaps or pinnae changes in size depending on latitude. The Arctic fox (*Alopex lagopus*) is characterized by its relatively small ears, developed to minimize heat loss from the body, whereas the fennec fox (*Fennecus zerda*), found in desert areas, has very large ears giving an increased surface area for heat loss. Big ears also serve to trap sound waves very effectively, enabling small prey such as rodents to be detected with great accuracy. In large-eared species, hearing assumes increased importance for hunting purposes. Lack of aggression between these foxes also ensures that large ears are not a liability; otherwise they could be prone to injury as a result of fighting.

Keen eyesight is especially important for African wild dogs (*Lycaon pictus*) which hunt prey in relatively open terrain, while grey wolves (*Canis lupus*) (below) rely to a greater extent on their scenting skills in tracking quarry.

Keen hearing is important in the case of more social canids as well. They will communicate with each other by a series of howls from a distance, as well as yelping, and growling, which tends to be used at close quarters, in response to a threat. Interestingly, wild canids do not bark loudly like domestic dogs. The barking of wolves, for example, is a much quieter sound, often made when they are close to their den. Domestication has led to barking becoming a much louder, more frequent and challenging vocalization. Nevertheless, wolves can learn this sound and dingoes, with their domestic ancestry, still retain the ability to bark, typically after howling. Other, lower intensity sounds will be made when canids are in close contact with each other, such as murmurs which may act as a greeting.

It is well known that domestic dogs can hear over a much wider frequency range than their owners, and this applies also in the case of wild canids. This is clearly useful when detecting prey such as rodents which may communicate in the ultrasound range.

Of the species which have been studied, it appears that the coyote (*Canis latrans*) possesses the most sensitive hearing, with an upper limit of 80,000 Hz; that of the greyhound is approximately 60,000 Hz, just below the red fox (*Vulpes vulpes*), measured at 65,000 Hz. It is suspected that there may well be a wide spread within the Canidae, reflecting the relative significance of auditory stimuli for prey capture and communication purposes.

Being active both by day and night, canids need to be able to see effectively under a range of lighting conditions. This has led to the development in canids, as with most other carnivores, of an additional group of cells arranged

Red foxes (*Vulpes vulpes*) have acute hearing, which enables them to detect small prey such as rodents, and to sense approaching danger.

The ears of the Arctic fox (*Alopex lagopus*) are small, compared with those of the fennec fox (*Fennecus zerda*) (below). Ear size is important with regard to both heat loss and sound location, becoming larger in desert-dwelling canids.

in layers behind the retina. Called the tapetum lucidum, this serves to reflect back light which has passed through the retina without stimulating any receptor cells. In effect, it increases the light intensity, improving the quality of the image, and is the reason why dogs' eyes glow in the dark if a bright light is shone at them.

There are two different types of cell present on the retina, known as the rods and the cones. The rods are used for vision under conditions of low light intensity, whereas the cones provide the image during daylight, and are responsible for colour vision. It has been found that the colour vision of dogs is somewhat less highly developed than our own.

The position of the eyes on the head contributes to the dog's hunting skills, and has been refined in domestic breeds which have been developed for hunting purposes. In the first instance, dogs need a wide visual field, so as to have the greatest opportunity to detect possible prey. With eyes set wide on the front of the face, this may give a field of view of 270° out of a possible 360°. In comparison, humans can appreciate an area equivalent to just 100°.

Having pursued its prey up to the point of capture, a dog must rely upon its vision to assess the precise position of its target, relative to its own position, in order to launch a fatal strike. This is achieved by means of binocular vision, with the brain superimposing the overlapping images received via the optic nerves from each eye. Domestic breeds which hunt, such as the greyhound have a narrow snout, with their eyes positioned well forwards, whereas in round-faced breeds such as the bulldog, the field of vision is significantly reduced.

Smell

Even for species which inhabit relatively open countryside, and rely to a great extent on vision, there is no doubt that a keen sense of smell is crucial. Canids rely on odours not only for locating prey, but also as a means of communication between individuals, either directly by contact or indirectly by scent.

Most of the research carried out on the sense of smell in canids has been done using the domestic dog, but the results probably apply, at least to some degree, to all species. It is well known, for example, that bloodhounds can follow trails several days old and that dogs can detect the smell of carefully concealed drugs. Even so, it appears that the dog's ability is not actually the result of a greater ability to detect a range of scents, but rather to distinguish between them. The elongated shape of the snout is useful for this purpose, and its interior comprises scrolls of bone, called turbinates, which have a wide surface area. This area is also supplied with plenty of nerves so that information obtained here can then be transmitted in detail along the olfactory nerve to the brain.

The scents pass into the nose through the nostrils, which are incorporated into the leathery external portion of the nose, the rhinarium. This area is almost always moist and shiny, as the result of secretions from the lateral nasal glands, positioned towards the rear of the nasal chambers, opening about 2 cm (¾ in) from the nostrils. The nasolacrimal duct, which provides a passage for fluid from the eye down the nose, opens anteriorly to the lateral

Scent is important for communication purposes in all canids, such as this maned wolf (*Chrysocyon brachyurus*).

nasal gland, and thus also helps to keep the surface of the nose moist. In addition, canids can also lick their noses.

The dampness of the rhinarium serves to improve the canid's sense of smell by increasing the amount of moisture that is inhaled, along with the particles of scent. External factors that affect a dog's ability to follow a scent include hunger, which stimulates a more acute olfactory response, and consumption of fat, which appears to lead to a decreased sensitivity for a period of time. The scenting skills of canids also vary with age, those of newborn pups being most limited.

The nostrils are not rigid, round chambers forming part of the rhinarium. Instead, there are slits at their sides, which can be used to increase the volume of air being inhaled. By flaring their nostrils, dogs can draw in more air and potentially capture more scent molecules.

There is one further refinement to assist in detecting scents. This is the vomeronasal organ, which is in the form of a pouch and is located in the roof of the mouth. Also known as Jacobsen's organ, this structure is thought to be associated with odours relating to other members of the same species, and with feeding behaviour. Tracing the connections of Jacobsen's organ with the brain helps to give an insight into its likely function. In contrast to the nerves from the nasal region, which lead to the lateral part of the hypothalamus, the nerves from Jacobsen's organ connect with the medial hypothalamus and the medial pre-optic area, which are concerned with mating behaviour. They also link to the ventro-medial nucleus in the brain, which is involved in feeding behaviour, notably its cessation.

The nose of wild canids is normally moist, to assist in the detection of scents, as shown by this grey fox (*Urocyon cinereoargenteus*). The golden jackal (*Canis aureus*) (below) is licking its nose to keep it moist.

Wild dogs drink using their tongue to lap up water, as shown by this grey wolf (*Canis lupus*). This acts rather like a ladle.

Assuming that the dog eats the most palatable food available first, there may be some relationship between declining appetite, as the stomach becomes full, and the food being eaten, so that ultimately, the dog's food requirement becomes satiated, and it stops eating. Jacobsen's organ may help to convey information about the food to the hypothalamus, where this is co-ordinated with input about the amount of food present in the stomach.

As in other animals, the senses of smell and taste in the dog are almost inextricably linked, of course. The distribution of the taste buds on the tongue varies somewhat between species, although there are always taste buds which respond to sour foods present over the entire surface of the tongue. Those which respond essentially to salty tastes can be found at the back and sides, while sweet flavours are detected on the edges, as well as towards the tip of the tongue.

The tongue itself is a mobile structure, whose musculature permits it to be used rather like a ladle, for drinking purposes. When the tip is curved, this serves to lap up water, which is then flicked to the back of the mouth and swallowed. This process is repeated quickly, maintaining the flow of water. Although dogs do not naturally suck up fluids, they can learn to do so as an alternative, if their tongue becomes paralysed.

Scent-marking

Glandular secretions are used as a method of communication between canids, either when two individuals meet, for example, or by scent-marking within a territory. On the dorsal surface of the tail, the so-called violet gland can be

49

found in most, although apparently not all, species of canid. This structure is named after the smell of the secretion produced – it was said to resemble violets when it was first described in foxes. The actual odour may differ somewhat according to the species, however, being described as pungent and not dissimilar to musk in the case of the grey fox (*Urocyon cinereoargenteus*), for example.

The violet gland enlarges in size at the outset of the breeding season, and is bigger in females than males. Its presence in some species may be highlighted by darker hair, as in the case of the fennec fox (*Fennecus zerda*), and the grey fox, where it is particularly large. In the grey fox there is no underfur covering the gland, and the guard hairs are black at their tips. In contrast, the gland is absent in the African wild dog (*Lycaon pictus*), and probably the maned wolf (*Chrysocyon brachyurus*) as well.

The secretion of the anal glands serves to give a characteristic individual odour to the faeces. The internal anal sacs are relatively small, opening on each side and just below the anus. The glandular secretions are conveyed from here via ducts onto the faeces. This enables other canids to recognize the dog concerned, and allows it to use its faeces as a territorial marker, often depositing it in a prominent position within its range.

Urine is also used as a territorial marker in canids, and this can trigger a process called flehmening when an individual encounters the scent of another of the same species. Most characteristically the lips are pulled back in a grimace for a moment. Although such behaviour has not been observed in all species of canid, there is no doubting the social importance of scent, even in those which generally lead solitary lives.

THERMOREGULATION

Canids do not have eccrine sweat glands over the surface of their bodies. Instead, these are concentrated between the toes, and would appear to be of little value in assisting thermoregulation, in view of their limited distribution. It is thought that these glands may be more significant in depositing scent, with those present between the pads of the Arctic fox (*Alopex lagopus*) said to have a powerful odour.

The apocrine glands, distributed elsewhere on the body, apart from the rhinarium, help to produce the characteristic body odour, which may be particularly strong in the case of the red fox (*Vulpes vulpes*), for example, but have no thermoregulatory value. Instead, the lateral nasal glands (see page 46) are again involved in this process. At a moderate temperature, canids will breathe in and out through the nose, and the evaporation of moisture helps to cool the body.

In hotter conditions, however, they start to pant with their mouths open, breathing in through the nose and out through the mouth. This provides the most effective means of keeping cool, with the greatest evaporation occurring during inspiration. In turn, as the temperature of the air rises, the lateral nasal glands secrete fluid at a higher rate, thus maximizing the efficiency of this cooling system.

The body itself is primarily designed to restrict heat loss, the fur providing excellent insulation for this purpose. The thick underfur of the Arctic fox, for

When they are hot, dogs such as this New Guinea singing dog, will pant to cool themselves down.

The Arctic fox (*Alopex lagopus*) is able to survive at temperature as low as −60°C (−76°F) without apparent discomfort. Curling round into a ball enables it to keep warmer than if it lay on its side.

example, enables it to live without apparent discomfort at temperatures as low as −60°C (−76°F). Arctic foxes can also reduce the blood flow to the skin in cold weather, minimizing direct heat loss from the skin. All canids can also adjust the amount of insulation provided by the fur to some extent by holding it sleek against the body in warmer weather, or fluffing it up to trap more air in colder conditions. They can also keep warm during cold nights by curling up in a ball to sleep, tucking their thinly coated legs into their body.

COMMUNICATION

While some members of the Canidae live essentially on their own, others, such as the African wild dog (*Lycaon pictus*), are highly social by nature. Direct long-range communication between individuals is based on vocalizations. The larger canids such as grey wolves (*Canis lupus*) have little to fear by revealing their presence. Howling helps group members to stay in touch with each other, and also appears to unify a pack; once one wolf starts howling, others will respond in a similar fashion.

Although the calls may sound similar to us, each member of the pack can be distinguished by its call. This helps to ensure that outsiders do not penetrate the pack's territory. In fact, howling by the members of one pack often leads to a sequence in which neighbouring packs also participate. This level of communication ensures that no territorial incursions or conflicts occur.

More solitary species such as red foxes (*Vulpes vulpes*) may call in a more aggressive manner to deter potential rivals. Study of their calls has revealed that again, individuals can be recognized by their distinctive intonations. They bark most often in the winter months, leading up to the mating period, especially on cold, moonlit nights. This is the time when scenting conditions are relatively poor.

African wild dogs (*Lycaon pictus*) are very determined pack hunters. They are well-built for speed and stamina, although their front legs may appear rather slender.

Wild canids can be found in a wide range of habitats. A number of species, such as the maned wolf (*Chrysocyon brachyurus*), tend to inhabit open areas of grassland, whereas the grey wolf (*Canis lupus*) (below) may be more at home in woodland.

Wolves frequently howl to keep in touch with other pack members. They may also play together on a regular basis.

Less noisy calls may have more localized purposes, such as a vixen warning her cubs of danger. They are nevertheless able to respond in adult fashion, barking if necessary from an early age.

One of the most remarkable voices in the canid family is that of the dhole (*Cuon alpinus*), also known as the whistling hunter. Tracking prey in undergrowth, these dogs utter a howling whistle which they use to keep in touch with each other while encircling quarry, ensuring that the strike, when it comes, is co-ordinated. This is especially important when they are attacking potentially dangerous prey. In common with other canids, dholes do not possess a lethal bite, and must therefore overcome their quarry by combining their physical strength.

At close quarters with each other, dogs rely on a series of facial gestures to convey their mood and intentions, usually in conjunction with movements of their tail and ears. If the dog adopts a low posture, with its ears down and tail held firmly between its legs, this is a gesture of submission. The lips in this case are held horizontally. Should a challenge occur, the submissive individual is likely to respond by rolling over on its back.

In an aggressive or challenging mood, canids attempt to make themselves look larger and more intimidating by raising their hackles – the area of hair running along the back, above the shoulders – so that the hair is vertical. The ears are also raised, and the lips are pulled back, baring the teeth, with the tail extended horizontally or lifted.

The calls of the red fox (*Vulpes vulpes*) can carry a considerable distance at night, when it is most likely to be heard.

When greeting another member of the pack, the dog is likely to wag its tail, and pull its lips back in a grin. If it is feeling in a playful mood, then it will lower its forelegs and spring up, encouraging a response from its companion. They may then chase off together, before pausing and repeating these movements.

Scent is important for recognition purposes; canids frequently sniff each other in the peri-anal region, where the anal sacs discharge their pungent secretion. Some species, such as the red fox (*Vulpes vulpes*) may use their faeces at least for part of the year for marking territory. Other canids, such as the dhole (*Cuon alpinus*), which live communally, appear less inclined to do this, although they may deposit their faeces in obvious areas, often having dunging sites, used by a number of individuals. The dens inhabited by dholes are never soiled, and these dunging areas are invariably some distance away. They are normally used when a hunting party sets out, rather than being at the borders of their territory. This tends to suggest that they have no role in marking an area.

All male wild canids urinate by raising one of their hindlegs and directing their urine in a horizontal direction, although submissive individuals in a pack may squat. Bitches may also occasionally urinate like males, rather than squatting. This is particularly common during the oestrus period. Young canids of both sexes will squat before attaining puberty.

It has been noted that male red foxes (*Vulpes vulpes*) may also adopt this posture to mark a relatively horizontal surface. Both new and established sites may be used for scent-marking in this fashion. Perhaps not surprisingly, this behaviour occurs more commonly during the mating season, and is also relatively frequent in snowy weather, when more familiar territorial land-marks may be hidden.

The dhole (*Cuon alpinus*) is also known as the whistling hunter, because of the calls made by pack members as they close in on their quarry.

Close communication calls for a series of facial gestures and movements, as shown by these African wild dogs (*Lycaon pictus*).

The significance of urine for scent-marking in some members of the family is less clear-cut. It is suspected that the dhole (*Cuon alpinus*) does not use its urine for marking either territorial boundaries or particular paths. In other social species, direct communication between individuals is likely to be of more significance, decreasing reliance on scent-marking of this type. Solitary canids, living at relatively low densities, are most likely to benefit from such scents. They are probably able to determine both the sex of the animal and its frequency of visitation to the spot by means of scent.

TERRITORIES AND PREY

The density of canids in an area is determined to a large extent by the availability of suitable food. Where this is readily available, the territories will be relatively small. This is exemplified by the case of the grey wolf (*Canis lupus*). Grey wolf packs may occupy areas ranging from as little as 100 km^2 (36 square miles) up to 10,000 km^2 (3600 square miles), and may vary in size from single pairs up to large aggregates of over 20 individuals. The ease with which prey can be caught is a major influence on the size of the pack: in parts of North America where moose (*Alces alces*) form an important prey species, wolves occur in larger packs. The size of the pack may also vary during the year; groups tend to split up during the spring and summer, when smaller prey is more likely to be available for them.

The social structure within packs of African wild dogs (*Lycaon pictus*) is well-developed, providing further support for the theory that as canids increase in size, so the tendency for them to associate together in packs becomes stronger.

Wild canids are naturally inquisitive by nature, as shown by this grey fox (*Urocyon cinereoargenteus*). This can prove fatal for them on occasions.

The fennec fox (*Fennecus zerda*) regularly feeds on rodents.

Wild dogs usually hunt together, but when food is short, they will scavenge on carrion. As in the case of other widely distributed species, there may be distinct variations in their normal prey. On the plains of East Africa, Thompson's gazelles (*Gazella thomsoni*) are most commonly killed, while in the Kruger National Park, the impala (*Aepyceros melampus*) is their major prey species. Nevertheless, packs can also cope with larger quarry such as zebra (*Equus burchelli*), which may weigh up to 200 kg (440 lb).

Some canids will hunt in water if necessary, and they can certainly swim, should this be required. Bush dogs (*Speothos venaticus*) are the most aquatic species, and may prey upon pacas (*Agouti* spp.), rodents that spend much of their time browsing on aquatic vegetation, seizing them in the water.

Hunting techniques vary according to the species. With little or no cover available, African hunting dogs must adopt a direct approach to potential quarry, relying on teamwork to achieve a kill. Once the animal is alerted and attempts to break away, the pack members follow in pursuit. Some dogs are able to run on a more direct line, and may ultimately take over the chase from the initial leaders. The quarry is finally knocked off balance on the ground, and before it can recover, the dogs rip open the unfortunate animal's underparts, eviscerating it. This killing technique is crude, in contrast to the lethal neck bite employed by lions.

Occurring in open terrain, wild dogs locate and pursue their target mainly by sight, whereas wolves may have to rely more on their sense of smell. They can locate animals up to 2.5 km (1½ miles) away by this means, although they are usually much closer.

Stealth is a more important aspect of the wolf's hunting technique. Pack members try to move in as close as possible before launching a strike, and, by approaching from upwind, may get to within 10 m (30 ft) of their target before being detected.

Deer are able to outrun a pack of wolves, provided that they detect the danger early enough. Wolves will not pursue quarry over long distances, with chases of 8 km (5 miles) being exceptional. Whereas deer pose little threat to wolves, an adult moose is a dangerous proposition. It may decide to stand its ground when threatened, charging at the nearest wolves, before swinging round to prevent an attack from the rear. The wolves may then attempt to push home the challenge, but are simply hoping to encourage the moose to flee, which will give them a better chance of overcoming it.

Even so, an adult moose can still outrun a pack of wolves, or may pause again and stand its ground. The moose will be at its most vulnerable if attacked on the run, as its injuries will then slow it down, with the wolves concentrating on its flanks and rump at this stage. Several will then close in, and leap at the throat, and the nose, pulling the animal down to the ground.

The hunting success of wolves, however, is well below that of African hunting dogs. According to one study involving a wolf pack in the Isle Royale National Park, where moose form a major prey species, they achieved just a 5 per cent success rate in terms of kills. It becomes easier for wolves to achieve a kill when they come upon a mother and calf, although the female moose will launch into a determined defence of her offspring. In this case, the pack attempts to distract the female, while other members of the group close in on the calf.

Overall, wolves rarely kill healthy, mature animals. Rather, they prey upon weakened or young individuals. As a preliminary move, both grey wolves and African wild dogs will often test their potential quarry, and try to identify a slower or otherwise incapacitated individual. This animal then becomes their target, to the virtual exclusion of those around it. By this means, a kill can be attained with minimum effort.

Other canids may engage in a less active manner of obtaining food. Jackals are essentially scavengers, adept at stealing from the kills of other carnivores, or searching through discarded garbage, although they will hunt on occasions. On the Serengeti plains, jackals will prey directly on Thompson's gazelles, and also hunt around the dung heaps, looking for beetles. Where there is more cover available, rodents and birds tend to replace beetles as prey, at least in the case of the black-backed jackal (*Canis mesomelas*), while the golden jackal (*C. aureus*), which also occurs here, takes more invertebrates.

Further evidence of the adaptability of jackals can be seen from other parts of their range. Whereas in Serengeti scavenging is rare, this feeding behaviour becomes more significant in Ngorongoro, since jackals are confronted here by larger prey than gazelles, in the form of wildebeest (*Connochaetes* spp.). They then rely on kills made by larger predators, although during the wildebeest calving period they will consume the remains of afterbirth. At other times of the year, the jackals feed on fruit, and also kill snakes.

A remarkable case of adaptive hunting was recorded in Kenya, where a female jackal was observed on a number of occasions running in among game. This enabled a waiting female cheetah (*Acinonyx jubatus*) to move closer, and

Pack size has a direct influence on the hunting abilities of African wild dogs (*Lycaon pictus*). It has declined significantly in recent years.

A pair of bush dogs (*Speothos venaticus*) on the alert.

Stealth is an important part of the canid hunting technique, displayed here by a maned wolf (*Chrysocyon brachyurus*) (above), while a golden jackal (*Canis aureus*) (below) may prefer to seek out carrion while remaining alert to hunting possibilities.

make a successful kill. She then fed on the carcass with her offspring, with the jackal and her pups taking over once the cheetahs had left. Prior to the development of this unusual hunting alliance, it is probable that the jackal had already been scavenging on cheetah kills in the area.

Jackals themselves are most likely to hunt together when they have pups, and so require more food. Any surplus from a kill will be carried off and buried, out of reach of scavengers, and consumed soon afterwards. Many canids will cache food in a similar way.

Smaller canids are adaptable in terms of their diet, although rodents and lagomorphs feature prominently as favoured prey items. Birds may also be taken, especially those such as pheasants which breed on the ground. Scavenging is also important in some areas, such as Algonquin Park in the USA, where red foxes (*Vulpes vulpes*) feed on the remains of wolf kills, or in many urban cities, where they forage in sacks of rubbish for edible items.

The resourcefulness of the red fox is also apparent in areas where they have been introduced, as in Australia. Here in agricultural areas, sheep placentae are consumed avidly during the lambing season, while mice are taken in preference to rabbits. They will also prey upon marsupials, and take insects, when other sources of food are in short supply.

When myxomatosis was introduced to Britain in 1953, the initial impact on the rabbit population was devastating. It is thought that over 95 per cent of rabbits were wiped out, and such a drastic and sudden reduction of their natural prey might have had an equally serious impact on the fox population

Wolves develop a hunting strategy which is best-suited to their prey, but even so, many hunting attempts end in failure.

Having obtained food, jackals must try to make sure that it is not stolen by other larger predators such as hyaenas. This is a golden jackal (*Canis aureus*).

The red fox (*Vulpes vulpes*) – one of the most adaptable of all canids when it comes to obtaining food.

as well. Nevertheless, studies from that era reveal that foxes again adapted, taking more voles and birds to compensate for the relative shortage of rabbits. There are some indications that foxes do have some distinct feeding preferences, however; when other foods are also available, they will still consume apples and other fruits, as well as berries.

Other species of fox are equally adaptable in their feeding habits, with their diet closely reflecting their environment, and being influenced by the season in many cases. This applies particularly in the case of the Arctic fox (*Alopex lagopus*), where scavenging along the shore provides a ready source of food, which is supplemented with birds' eggs and fledglings through the brief summer and then berries in the autumn. During the harsh northern winter these foxes frequently cache food, returning to eat it when other food is in short supply. Such stores may contain sufficient food to last a fox for up to a month.

Although foxes in general have acquired a reputation for stealing poultry, the majority of species do not prey to any great extent on domestic stock. A study of 37 Cape foxes (*Vulpes chama*) confirmed that they were no threat to livestock. Rodents and insects, along with carrion were identified in the stomach contents, but no remains of poultry were found.

Several species of fox have more specialized diets. The bat-eared fox (*Otocyon megalotis*) is largely insectivorous, digging into termite nests to obtain its food, although again, it will scavenge. The crab-eating fox (*Cerdocyon thous*) certainly does feed on crabs, although these would appear to form only a limited part of its diet. Investigations in Venezuela have revealed that rodents are again the favoured prey of this species, while frogs, lizards and turtle eggs all feature in its diet.

More aquatic items are caught by the raccoon dog (*Nyctereutes procyonoides*), including water beetles and fish, although again, there is a seasonal variation in diet. Frogs are taken predominantly when they congregate in ponds during the springtime when they are breeding. Fish are also caught in greater numbers as they head up rivers to their traditional spawning sites.

Scavenging becomes more important in the autumn or winter, although in the harshest parts of their range, raccoon dogs will hibernate to conserve their reserves of food. A noticeable weight gain is then likely to be apparent in the autumn, as the raccoon dogs build up fat reserves to last them over the winter period.

Generalizations in physical characteristics and dietary requirements have ensured that canids can be found in a wide variety of habitats today. They are well-placed to exploit a changing environment, as shown by the increasing penetration of the red fox (*Vulpes vulpes*) into urban areas.

Only human influence, and diseases such as rabies and distemper have exerted any serious threat to their numbers. If one prey species becomes scarce, canids can transfer to another or resort to a diet based increasingly on fruit and vegetables for a period. The implications for the conservation of wild canids is clear-cut. Provided that human persecution pressures can be lifted, an endangered population should be able to recover with minimal assistance.

Chapter 3
Reproduction

The social structure of the Canidae is influenced markedly by the size of the species concerned. At the smaller end of the scale, most foxes tend to be monogamous, occurring in individual pairs, although some males may mate with more than one female during the breeding period. Definite monogamy is usually observed in jackals and coyotes, whereas in wolves and the African hunting dog (*Lycaon pictus*), there is a tendency for females to mate with more than one partner during the course of the year.

Within a pack, however, there is again likely to be only one breeding pair. This is usual in the case of the grey wolf (*Canis lupus*), where the dominant pair prevent other members of the pack from mating. Other females in the pack display normal oestrus behaviour and undergo what is described in domestic dogs as 'phantom pregnancies'. This results in them producing milk at the same time as the dominant female, enabling them to act as surrogate mothers, if the female dies. They will also assist with this task under normal circumstances.

Yet the bonds within a wolf pack are not rigid. They tend to strengthen during the winter, when hunting may become more dangerous, and loosen at the onset of spring, and at this time some subordinate pairs may breed on their own. The basic unit of a pack stems from a breeding pair and their offspring, although the quarry of the pack influences the number of wolves in the pack.

In the case of the African hunting dogs, the female is the dominant member of the pack, living in the company of mature males and yearlings. These assist in providing food for the pups: without such help, the numbers of cubs surviving is low, in spite of the fact that females produce relatively large litters.

The imbalanced sex ratio in these packs seems to begin at birth. For some reason, more male than female pups are born, thus perpetuating the unusual social structure. In addition, female hunting dogs often leave the pack of their birth, whereas males are accepted into it. On occasions, however, a female may challenge her mother for dominance within the pack and, if successful, she then assumes dominance. Within a pack of hunting dogs, as with wolves, mating of subordinates is actively discouraged and cubs born to a subordinate are likely to be killed.

THE BREEDING PERIOD AND MATING

Unlike most domestic dogs, wild canids generally only breed once rather than twice during the year. In northern areas, this period is closely linked to the season, so that the young are born during the spring or early summer. This is likely to be the most favourable period for their survival, with food more readily obtainable.

Within groupings of wild canids there is a strict social ranking, and usually only the dominant pair breed, although other members of the pack often assist in the rearing of the young.

Breeding behaviour is conditioned by changes in daylength in temperate areas, although in the tropics there also appears to be a seasonality in terms of the reproductive cycle. Increased aggression, related to territorial claims, can often be observed at this stage, and scent-marking also becomes more frequent.

In many wild canids, the pair bond is formed some time before copulation, although initially, the female may be reluctant to take a partner. They may even fight at first, before the female signals her acceptance, although the actual sequence of events depends to a great extent on the individuals concerned.

The male will be drawn to sniff the female's genital region, with the female's body language indicating whether or not he will be accepted. These behavioural changes are mirrored by physiological changes in the female's body.

The initial stage in the oestrus cycle is described as pro-oestrus with the vulva becoming larger in size, and some blood loss becoming apparent in most but not all cases. This is not the equivalent of menstruation in primates, however, since it occurs prior to ovulation. The bitch becomes increasingly seductive during this phase, although she will not allow her partner to mate with her yet. This occurs during the subsequent oestrus period.

Bitches often become more playful as the oestrus period proceeds, prior to ovulation. This is an African wild dog (*Lycaon pictus*).

The penis in male canids is strengthened by means of a bone, called the baculum. The erectile tissue still has an important function, however, at the base of the glans. Here it is arranged in the shape of a ring, which swells during copulation, resulting in the so-called 'tie', which is characteristic of canid matings.

The male mounts his partner, clasping the sides of her body, in front of the hips, using his front legs. Soon after penetration, the bulb of the penis increases in size, with the constrictor muscles in the vaginal walls serving to anchor the penis firmly in place, preventing withdrawal.

The mating process proceeds through several distinct stages. Ejaculation of the spermatozoa occurs quite early during the tie, and once this has taken place, the male releases his grip on the female's body and the pair shift position, although they still remain tied together. The male shifts one of his hindlegs over her body, so that their hindquarters are together, with the dogs facing in opposite directions. This gives them both good visibility at this vulnerable time.

Secretions from the prostrate gland are released during this second stage of mating, helping to nourish the spermatozoa and assist their passage through the female reproductive tract. Only once the male's erection subsides can withdrawal occur.

There are individual variations on this process, however, depending upon the species. It appears that a tie occurs in all cases, although this may be a brief affair in the African wild dog (*Lycaon pictus*), lasting on average between 1 and 3 minutes, and never more than 5 minutes. In other species, mating may take from about 6 minutes in the raccoon dog (*Nyctereutes procyonoides*) up to 2 hours or so in the case of the grey wolf (*Canis lupus*).

Scent-marking is an important feature of communication between wild canids. Males may ascertain the readiness of a female to mate in this fashion. A maned wolf (*Chrysocyon brachyurus*) is shown here, sniffing the ground.

Mating is a brief encounter in the case of African wild dogs (*Lycaon pictus*), and only the dominant pair are likely to breed.

It is probably no coincidence that the mating process is quicker in the smaller species, which would be most vulnerable to predation. In the case of the African wild dog, a long static encounter would leave them vulnerable to the large predators such as lions, with which they share their habitat.

The function of the tie, which is not necessary to stimulate ovulation, is unclear, although it has been suggested that it may assist in determining the parentage of the offspring. After receiving spermatozoa, the reproductive tract of the female loses its receptivity to them shortly after mating. This means that provided a male can prevent the female from mating again soon afterwards, it is likely that his spermatozoa will actually fertilize her ova, even if she subsequently copulates with another partner.

In any event, as oestrus progresses, so the appeal of the bitch to dogs gradually declines. It is clear from domestic dogs that chemical messengers known as pheromones present in the vaginal secretions, and possibly in the urine and anal glands at this stage, attract the male to the bitch. One particular chemical, called methyl *p*-hydroxybenzoate, has been identified as triggering the male dog to mount the bitch.

GESTATION

Actual ovulation occurs early during the oestrus period, thus ensuring that eggs are available to be fertilized when mating takes place. If this does not prove successful, however, some females – especially female wolves – may undergo a pseudopregnancy. This results from changes in the ovary, and in particular the corpora lutea, which produce the hormone progesterone after the release of ova from the ovary. Normally, the corpora lutea stop producing progesterone if mating is unsuccessful or does not take place. Sometimes, however, they continue to produce the hormone and this results in a so-called 'phantom pregnancy' with swelling of the mammary glands, and even the production of milk in the absence of any pups.

The gestation period in wild canids is somewhat variable, being shortest in the foxes, averaging around 52 days in the red fox (*Vulpes vulpes*) for example. Pregnancy lasts about 9 weeks in the grey wolf (*Canis lupus*), while that of the African wild dog (*Lycaon pictus*) can extend between 72 and 80 days, which is the longest period of all canids.

There are three distinct stages in the development of the pregnancy after fertilization. First, the ova progress from the oviducts down into the uterus where they implant. This may not occur until nearly a third of the pregnancy has elapsed. The uterine horns in canids are relatively long, in contrast to the body, because litter size is quite large, and there must be adequate space to accommodate the developing pups.

Although the data on litter sizes in canids are somewhat restricted, and based largely on zoological records, it would appear that the maned wolf (*Chrysocyon brachyurus*) has the smallest litters, ranging from just a single pup up to a maximum of three. This can be correlated to the number of teats – female maned wolves have only two pairs. Other species may show much more variation in the number of offspring in a litter. African wild dogs rank among the most prolific, with as many as 16 being born in a single litter, while grey wolves and red foxes have been known to produce as many as 11, although 5 or 6 appears to be the average number in these two species. Female African wild dogs may have 14 nipples to nourish their offspring, with other species possessing between 8 and 10, although this is not a constant figure, even between individuals of the same species.

After the ova have implanted, the embryo starts to develop, along with the placenta. The organs are formed during this stage, but there is relatively little growth in terms of size of the pups. Finally, in the final third of pregnancy, they develop as foetuses. This progression is of value to the bitch, since it means that she will not have to carry the extra weight of her offspring until relatively close to the end of the gestation period. Up to this point therefore, she will be able to hunt and move without difficulty.

The canine placenta, responsible for nourishing a pup, actually wraps around the amnion surrounding the foetus, and is described as a belt placenta. Green staining is a feature associated with it, and is the result of the breakdown of the female's blood cells.

BIRTH AND EARLY DEVELOPMENT

As the time for giving birth approaches, the bitch is likely to retire to a den, which has been dug previously, and may already have been used as a retreat. These are well-concealed. In some cases, wild canids will take over the dens of other species, such as porcupines. There may be one or more entrances, and even several interconnecting dens.

The site chosen for the den appears to be influenced by the environment. Dholes (*Cuon alpinus*) may adopt a site in a dry river bank, or seek more

71

African wild dogs (*Lycaon pictus*) are potentially the most prolific of all species of wild canid, with females sometimes giving birth to 14 pups. In comparison, maned wolves (*Chrysocyon brachyurus*) (below) may have just two in a single litter.

seclusion in scrub. Groups may live together; one such community occupied an extensive den in a dry creek. It had six entrances, and more than 30 m (100 ft) of connecting tunnels. Generations of cubs would have been reared by their mothers here, although when discovered, the site was not in use.

There is also evidence that the dogs use the area around the den for playing. Cubs may develop their hunting skills here, using tunnels in long grass, for example, for ambush practice. Food is brought to the vicinity of the den, but inside, the chambers and tunnels are clean. The mother will eat her offsprings' faeces, while a dunging area for older animals will be nearby. In some cases, however, a plague of fleas in the den may cause a group to move on to a new site. Fleas breed in the vicinity of their hosts, rather than on them, and by abandoning the site, so the dogs can reduce the level of infestation.

Wild canids sometimes share their denning area with other animals, some of which may even be their natural prey. There are records of rabbits, for example, sharing the quarters of dingoes (*Canis familiaris dingo*), although whether this state of tolerance would continue if food was short is open to doubt.

Much still remains to be learnt about the early life of many species of wild dog, but the development of pups appears to follow a consistent pattern. At birth, the young are helpless. Each moves down the birth canal, wrapped in its allanto-chorionic sac filled with amniotic fluid. This may rupture during the birth process, although the bitch will lick it vigorously, breaking the membrane once the sac reaches her vulva. She will then bite through the amnion, in order to reach the cub. Vigorous licking stimulates the young dog to commence breathing. Soon after, the placenta will be expelled from the body, with the discharge of greenish fluid appearing at this stage.

Canids generally retreat to a den to give birth. An Arctic fox (*Alopex lagopus*) is portrayed here, in its summer coat.

The whole process may take between 2 and 6 hours, although it can be longer in some cases with a large litter. On average, there is likely to be an interval of 15 to 30 minutes between the appearance of each pup, but this may be extended if the litter is small.

After being licked clean, the young dogs will start suckling almost immediately. This is a strong instinct, and vital to their well-being, as they acquire colostrum from their mother at this stage. This so-called 'first milk', produced for the first 2 days of the pups' life, provides essential antibodies to protect them from infection until their own immune systems are fully competent. They do not develop the strict teat order seen in some other carnivores, such as cats, but they often display a preference for the rear teats close to the inguinal region.

At first they feed regularly every couple of hours or so, with this interval gradually extending to 4 hours by the time they are a week old. The youngsters use their hindlimbs to push against the mother's body, kneading the teats with their forelegs when they start to feed. This is sometimes described as milk-treading, and presumably stimulates the flow of milk from the glands.

Afterwards, they huddle together in order to conserve their body heat as they are unable to regulate their body temperature. All young dogs are therefore helpless, as well as blind, at birth. The fat content of canid milk is relatively high, which helps the cubs to maintain their body warmth using the heat produced by the breakdown of the fats. Interestingly, it appears that this applies even in species originating from warmer latitudes, indicating that the Canidae evolved in the north, and have subsequently moved into more tropical areas. Fat levels approaching 11 per cent have been recorded in the case of the grey wolf (*Canis lupus*), with a typical protein content of around 10 per cent.

The bitch will remain with her offspring almost constantly for the first few days. They cannot see or hear for up to a fortnight after being born, and are totally helpless, incapable of even wagging their tails at this stage. Most of their time is spent sleeping, although they can move slowly, crawling and lifting their heads to locate their mother in the den. The young dogs are not able to urinate or defecate independently at first, but are dependent on the licking action of their mother to stimulate this involuntary reflex. She keeps the den clean by consuming their faecal matter.

The development of young canids follows largely the same course in all species. The young usually open their eyes by the time they are just over a fortnight old. The female then starts to spend less time with her litter, as they grow older. Solid food is introduced to their diet by the time the youngsters are about a month old. Licking the face of their mother encourages her to regurgitate partially digested food for the cubs. Smaller species generally carry food to their pups. The mother's milk supply starts to decline at this stage, and she is less ready to allow the young dogs to suckle from her.

It is at this stage that helpers are especially useful in rearing the offspring, as their food demands increase significantly. Weaning is generally completed when the young are about 2 months old. Most young canids are then fully independent after a similar interval. While weaning occurs in the area where they were born, the female may sometimes transfer the pups to another den

Only once the pups are able to move freely will they emerge above ground. They will then form a family group, as shown by these young grey wolves (*Canis lupus*).

within her home range, occasionally moving more than once. This may be because heavy rainfall is threatening to lead to flooding of the burrow, or because the den is overrun with fleas. Shifting the locality of the young will also help to protect them from predators. Golden jackals (*Canis aureus*) have been observed to move their pups as many as five times in the first 3 months of life. Adults usually carry their offspring by holding them by the scruff of the neck, where the skin is relatively loose, leaving the body dangling in mid-air. The pups do not generally struggle when being moved in this fashion.

The dispersal of young depends to a great extent on the species concerned. In the case of the coyote (*Canis latrans*), for example, young may remain with their parents through to the end of the following year, assisting with the rearing of the next litter of pups. The same often applies in the case of jackals.

THE HELPER SYSTEM
The value of helpers extends well beyond the acquisition of additional food. They enable the mother to spend longer with her pups, rather than having to search for food. In addition, when she does go hunting, a helper will watch over the youngsters, protecting them from potential predators such as hyaenas. Otherwise, after 3 weeks of almost constant nursing, the young may be left on their own for nearly 10 hours every day.

The young are at their most vulnerable once they emerge from the den. A watchful helper can alert them to danger, encouraging them to take cover, and may also be able to drive off a predator intent on attack.

The significance of the helper system has been studied in the case of the side-striped jackal (*Canis adustus*). A pair on their own are likely to rear just one pup successfully, but this figure rises by the equivalent of nearly two for each helper. Up to six pups have been raised successfully by a pair assisted by three helpers.

Other factors which affect the survival of cubs may not be mitigated to the same extent by the presence of helpers. This has been shown in the golden jackal (*Canis aureus*), which whelps during the wet period. More cubs then die as the result of exposure and illness, rather than falling victim to predators and starvation, which the helper system is best equipped to overcome. Even so, many pairs of golden jackals have helpers accompanying them.

Strength in numbers can assist to protect food sources – whereas a single jackal may well have difficulty in deterring a flock of vultures from descending on a carcass, this is not a problem where there is a group. Some can feed, while others drive off the birds, with co-operation of this type benefiting the entire group.

It does not appear that helpers routinely take over the adults' territory. They simply disperse after having been helpers, moving to other groups. This period may nevertheless serve to equip them to survive better when they finally venture off on their own.

Bat-eared foxes (*Otocyon megalotis*) appear to have a fairly loose breeding arrangement. They tend to live in individual pairs, but may also associate in breeding groups in some areas. It seems that the young may spend some time

The golden jackal (*Canis aureus*) may benefit from the assistance of helpers, often yearlings who are not breeding themselves, when there are young pups to care for and feed. Even when resting this jackal is alert, as shown by the position of its ears.

with their parents after becoming independent, but there is no evidence to suggest they assist in the rearing of a subsequent family.

In some cases, offspring will spend their entire lives in the pack of their birth. Male African wild dogs (*Lycaon pictus*) rarely stray, even once they are mature. In contrast, young bitches start to leave in groups, and join up with other male groupings, rather than staying with the pack. Once they are ready to breed, battles for dominance break out between sibling females, and having lived in harmony together up until this point, the victor is likely to force the others out of the pack.

This species is unusual in that there is a distinct imbalance in the sex ratios, and not just within the adults. Overall, nearly 6 out of every 10 African wild dogs born are male. The reason behind this unusual arrangement probably relates to the difficulties of rearing offspring in areas where food supplies may well prove to be sporadic. If a number of females within a pack were to breed, then there may well be fewer survivors, in terms of the cubs, because of a shortage of food. With only one female breeding, and a number of males assisting with the rearing of the cubs, resources are best targeted to achieve successful breeding, even under adverse conditions.

In spite of this, it has been noted that African wild dogs suffer remarkably high levels of cub mortality with over a third dying during their first year. Even in captivity a relatively high number of cubs are lost which indicates that factors other than food availability are involved.

HYBRIDIZATION

In many parts of the world, hybridization between domestic and wild dogs takes place, and this process has sometimes been actively encouraged. Deliberate hybridization between the grey wolf (*Canis lupus*) and the German shepherd dog (formerly known as the Alsatian) underlies the appearance of the breed known as the Saarlooswolfhond. Working in conjunction with a zoo in the Netherlands, Leendert Saarloos began this hybrid breeding programme during the 1930s. He held the view that the domestic dog had deteriorated in both health and stamina, and would benefit from the introduction of further fresh wolf blood.

His theory was rather weakened by the death of the first wolf from a viral illness, thought to have been contracted from a dog. But he persevered, only to find that the resulting domestic dog–grey wolf hybrids bred from a second pairing proved far more wayward than their pure domestic counterparts, and failed to respond well to training. They were strongly territorial by nature, retained a strong pack instinct and were keen to roam, as well as being shy of people.

Undeterred, however, Saarloos persisted with his plan and by the time of his death in 1969, these initial problems had been overcome to a great extent. Continued refinement, concentrating on German shepherd stock, led ultimately to recognition of this breed by the Dutch Kennel Club 6 years later, although such dogs are not widely kept.

The domestic dog, as a direct descendant of the grey wolf, can be mated back to it, as Saaroos showed, and fertile offspring result. In recent years, hybrids of this type have become alarmingly fashionable in the United States, where it is now estimated that there could be as many as 600,000 of them. Various northern breeds are favoured for such crosses – notably Eskimo dogs, Alaskan malamutes and Siberian huskies, because these generally have stable temperaments. Even so, the resulting hybrids typically show the same behavioural problems noted by Saarloos. Not surprisingly, some states, such as New York, have taken steps to ban the keeping of wolf hybrids.

While most crossings involving wolves are the result of deliberate matings, it is not uncommon for coyotes (*Canis latrans*) to seek out and mate with domestic dogs. Usually, it is male coyotes which pair with domestic bitches. The resulting offspring are often described as coydogs, with their appearance varying somewhat, depending on the breed of dog involved. Strangely perhaps, records of wolves and coyotes breeding together are very scarce, and wolves will often actually kill coyotes if given an opportunity. One successful pairing of this type did take place in the early part of the present century, however, at the Riverdale Park, Toronto, Canada. Two adult coyote–wolf hybrids bred here are preserved at the Royal Ontario Museum.

Comparison of coydogs and wolf hybrids suggests that the former may be more aggressive when they mature, although in some cases, they have proved trainable. Friendly towards people whom they know well, coydogs are otherwise likely to be timid. They frequently show clear signs of both parents, and are fertile, as well as being able to bark like a domestic dog.

When red wolves (*Canis rufus*) were more numerous, they frequently hybridized with coyotes, notably in the western area of their former range.

Dingoes (*Canis familiaris dingo*) also breed readily with domestic dogs (*Canis familiaris*), to whom they are closely related.

The cross-breeding of the grey wolf (*Canis lupus*) (above) with domestic dogs (*Canis familiaris*) is currently on the increase in certain parts of the USA in particular.

The coyote has also been crossed with the golden jackal (*Canis aureus*) experimentally, and there are reports that domestic dogs have also mated successfully with jackals. This is a particular worry in the case of the Simien jackal (*Canis simensis*), whose population now comprises less than 1000 individuals. Crosses between domestic dogs and members of other canid genera are, not surprisingly, rather suspect. Nevertheless, Charles Darwin was among those who stated that pairings with the crab-eating zorro (*Cerdocyon thous*) could give rise to pups, and other visitors to the northern part of South America have seen hunting dogs supposedly resulting from such unions, although precise descriptions are sketchy. The same applies to a reported successful mating between a fox terrier and Azara's zorro (*Dusicyon gymnocercus*).

Elsewhere in the world, matings between the dingo (*Canis familiaris dingo*) and the domestic dog in Australia are not uncommon. This is not surprising, given the close relationship between these canids. Sheep farmers report that these dingo crosses are less fearful and more ruthless than pure dingoes, as well as often proving harder to track. In some cases, however, dingoes have been known to kill domestic dogs. Again, male dingoes, which can breed throughout the year, tend to sire puppies with bitches of domestic stock, rather than vice versa. In contrast to the domestic dog, female dingoes have one rather than two periods of heat each year.

Artificial hybrids have been produced on fur farms between red foxes (*Vulpes vulpes*) and Arctic foxes (*Alopex lagopus*), although the offspring in such cases are invariably sterile. This is because of the differences in chromosome numbers between the species concerned. The Arctic fox has up to 52 chromosomes whereas the red fox has just 34, and the resulting hybrids have 43. Members of the genus *Canis* apparently possess more chromosomes (78) than other wild canids, although these data are available for barely half of the family. African wild dogs also have a diploid count of 78 chromosomes.

LIFESPAN

Relatively little has been documented about the longevity of canids in the wild. It is generally assumed to be 10 years or less, based partly on captive records. Swift foxes (*Vulpes velox*) have lived 13 years in zoological collections, but their normal lifespan may well be less than 4 years under normal conditions, where they are more likely to be exposed to disease, predation and starvation.

Hunting pressures in some areas are more acute than in others, and this is likely to reduce the average lifespan in that area. Epidemics of disease, notably viruses such as rabies, and the deadly bacterial ailment anthrax can devastate populations in a region, as has occurred in the case of the African wild dog (*Lycaon pictus*). Even as predatory species, life is hazardous for canids, with the smaller species themselves being susceptible to larger carnivores.

Chapter 4
Evolution and Distribution

As the era of the dinosaurs drew to a close at the end of the Cretaceous period, about 65 million years ago, there was a relative absence of large predatory species on the planet. At this stage, the mammals which existed were small in size and mainly insectivorous in their feeding habits.

Increasing specialization can be observed in the fossil record, however, and today's predatory groups, comprising the order Carnivora, had clearly started to emerge around 40 million years ago. The earliest origins of the canids can be traced back to the late Eocene era. Remains unearthed in North America from this period show that they were short-legged in appearance and more closely resembled mongooses and civets than present-day canids.

The earliest distinctive proto-canid, called *Hesperocyon*, had an elongated muzzle, a long tail, and a fairly slender body shape. Its legs were short, and it walked with a digitigrade action (on its toes). While overall, *Hesperocyon* may not have appeared to show a strong relationship with contemporary carnivores, key distinguishing characteristics were already apparent. The auditory bullae of the inner ear were ossified, rather than cartilaginous, and there was a horizontal partition evident across the bullae. A slight reduction in dentition was also apparent, with the last molar tooth absent in each upper jaw, so that there were 42 teeth present in the mouth. This still necessitated a relatively long muzzle in order to accommodate them.

Differences in the shape of the teeth were already obvious, confirming that *Hesperocyon* was a true carnivore. The shearing action was created by the first molar tooth in the lower jaw and the last premolar in the upper jaw, creating the carnassial cutting surface.

Right from the dawn of their history, canids have been relatively unspecialized hunters. *Hesperocyon*, for example, which grew to a length of about 80 cm (2½ ft) in length, not only hunted small mammals, but also almost certainly scavenged and ate vegetable matter, including fruit. It is not known whether they were social or solitary by nature, but since studies of contemporary canids suggest that hunting large prey is a major factor in the formation of packs, it seems likely that *Hesperocyon* was solitary, or may have lived in pairs.

Towards the later part of the Oligocene, other similar canids started to evolve in North America. But it was not until the close of the Eocene that canids began to spread further afield, to other continents.

The first canid which bore a clear resemblance to a modern member of the group was *Cynodesmus*. Its remains have been discovered in Nebraska, and it was not dissimilar to a coyote (*Canis latrans*) in appearance. The body of *Cynodesmus* was relatively long, however, as was its tail, and its legs were quite long, compared with other canids. The first toe on each foot, which have become the dew claws in contemporary canids, show a reduction in size, although they were still in contact with the ground at this stage. The claws themselves were thin in shape, and could be retracted, rather like those of a cat.

Cynodesmus probably hunted in a fashion not dissimilar from felids, ambushing rather than pursuing prey. At this stage, there was still plenty of cover available, with the Great Plains of North America not yet having developed. As a result, hunting could be carried out successfully using stealth, rather than pace.

Primitive canids were still evolving alongside *Cynodesmus. Phalocyon*, a contemporary genus also unearthed from early Miocene deposits in Nebraska, were probably rather similar to raccoons in appearance, and the structure of their limbs appears to have been more suited to climbing trees than running.

A third genus, *Osteoborus*, which first appeared somewhat later, during the late Miocene in the same part of the world, was primarily a scavenger rather than an active hunter. The origins of this group date back about 8 million years. They were stocky, heavily built dogs which filled an evolutionary niche similar to the hyaenas of today, and have become known as hyaena dogs. Their snout was short and square, with muscles giving considerable power to the jaws. Their carnassial teeth were able to crush the bones of carcasses, enabling them to extract the bone marrow, and the premolars were significantly enlarged for this purpose.

Other members of this group, which were known as borophagines, may well have been more predatory in their lifestyle. There is evidence that *Epicyon*, for example, lived in groups, and may have had a lifestyle not unlike that of today's wolves.

This lineage was ultimately to prove a blind alley, however, along the evolutionary pathway which has led to contemporary canids. Having first split off from the *Hesperocyon* lineage around 30 million years ago, the borophagines finally became extinct during the Pleistocene, about 1.5 million years ago, with *Osteoborus* itself being one of the last members of the group to disappear.

A second split had occurred at an early stage, during the Eocene about 10 million years before the emergence of the borophagines. This ultimately gave rise to the ancestor's of today's bears, and another branch which resulted in a group known as the amphicyonids or half-dogs (and sometimes, rather misleadingly, as bear-dogs).

While the development of the Canidae occurred in North America, that of the amphicyonids took place predominantly in Eurasia. *Amphicyon* itself was a large animal, thought to be somewhat similar to a bear in appearance. The structure of its teeth suggests that vegetable matter formed a significant part of its diet. This group was successful, and its remains have been found throughout the northern hemisphere.

Other amphicyonids were smaller in size. *Cynodictis*, for example, could well have been a scavenger, stealing from the kills of larger predators, in a similar way to jackals today. Indeed, there seems to have been considerable diversity in their appearance. Some forms which seem to have been more akin to cats than dogs have been discovered.

The earliest known appearance of amphicyonids in North America took place during the late Oligocene, about 30 million years ago, when they crossed the Bering land bridge. One of the most ferocious of the invaders was probably the giant half-dog (*Daphoenodon superbus*), whose remains have been found in early Miocene deposits of Nebraska.

These were large predators, which inhabited underground dens, where their remains have sometimes been discovered. While their bodies were bulky, like modern bears, their heads showed canine characteristics. They walked in a plantigrade fashion, using their entire feet, rather than just their toes. It appears that ultimately, *Daphoenodon* declined at the expense of *Amphicyon* itself, and had vanished by the middle of the Miocene.

The reasons for the extinction of the amphicyonids as a group is unclear. It may have been related to the appearance of wolves and bears, which were better suited to the climatic changes that were taking place at this stage. In any event, the amphicyonid lineage finally came to an end during the late Miocene, about 8 million years ago.

THE DEVELOPMENT OF TODAY'S DOGS

At the close of the Oligocene, the hesperocyonine dogs had developed into various forms. There were smaller canids, such as *Phaocyon*, which were at least partially frugivorous in their feeding habits, and more powerful forms, such as *Enhydrocyon*, able to hunt and scavenge effectively, with a dentition that enabled them to crush bones.

These groups all became extinct at this stage, however, and their evolutionary niches tended to be filled for a period by amphicyonids, until the late Miocene. During this epoch, true dogs journeyed across the Bering land bridge from North America to Asia, and the group was then able to radiate directly from here into Europe.

This critical stage in the evolution of the canids occurred between 5 and 7 million years ago. At this time, before the continents had separated, the temperature in this part of the world was higher than it is today, but even so, these early canids would have needed a dense coat to protect them from the cold.

The dogs which first settled in Asia are thought to have looked something like *Canis davisii*, which was about the size of a coyote. This is considered to be the prototype that ultimately gave rise to the two main lineages of dogs recognized today – the foxes and the wolves.

Prior to this division, however, it appears that there had been a separate event which saw the break-off of the ancestors of today's raccoon dog (*Nyctereutes procyonoides*). The grey fox (*Urocyon cinereoargenteus*) is believed to be derived from an even older separate lineage, which dates back between 6 and 9 million years.

ASIATIC DIVERSITY AND EXPANSION

The arrival of the early dogs in Asia occurred at an ideal time. An evolutionary niche was being created by climatic change, and at the same time those creatures, such as the amphicyonids, which could affect the spread of the dogs were becoming extinct.

The grey fox (*Urocyon cinereoargenteus*) has an evolutionary history which can be traced back at least 6 million years.

The earth's temperature had been falling throughout the Miocene and areas of woodland were being replaced by grassland. Herbivorous mammals had to adapt to a differing diet, with less emphasis on leaves, and were also faced with less cover in which to hide from potential predators.

Speed became more significant both for hunter and hunted alike, but by pursuing their quarry in packs, dogs were able to gain a vital advantage. The generalist and adaptable lifestyle of canids, which enables them to be omnivorous in their feeding habits, was probably a further factor which assisted their spread through Eurasia at this stage.

The slow-moving, well-protected mega-herbivores were gradually replaced by nimble animals, such as antelopes. In order to take advantage of such quarry, the lupine dogs developed pace, with the combined strength of the pack being able to overcome their prey. With individual dogs largely unable to inflict a fatal bite like cats, they were forced to rip their victims apart.

The success of their colonization of Eurasia can be gauged by the fact that canids had spread right across into Europe by the early Pleistocene, some 3 million years ago. Remains of various wolves, as well as a dhole, raccoon dog and *Vulpes* foxes have all been found here in strata from this era.

The red fox (*Vulpes vulpes*) was established at an early stage. In turn, it gave rise to the corsac fox (*V. corsac*), and then both Rüppell's fox (*V. rueppelli*) and the swift fox (*V. velox*). Africa presented no challenge to foxes, with the Cape fox (*V. chama*) reaching the tip of the continent. Members of the vulpine lineage, beginning with the bat-eared fox (*Otocyon megalotis*) also began to establish themselves here. As the Sahara desert started to form in North Africa around 4 million years ago, so the foxes adapted successfully to the severity of this climate. The fennec fox (*Fennecus zerda*) remains living proof of this process, as does Blanford's fox (*V. cana*) in the Middle East.

THE REINVASION OF THE AMERICAS

Having undergone a period of development in Eurasia, some canids moved back across the Bering land bridge into North America, before this link was lost. This is why, for example, the grey wolf (*Canis lupus*) occurred throughout the northern hemisphere, with the earliest remains from North America dating back some 700,000 years. Even earlier, about 2 million years ago, the hare-eating coyote (*Canis leptophagus*) had also travelled this same route, and is today considered to be the ancestor of today's coyote (*Canis latrans*). Red foxes (*Vulpes vulpes*) also established themselves in North America at this stage.

The Pleistocene saw three different lineages of wolf in North America: *C. lupus* and *C. rufus*, both of which still survive here today, and the dire wolf (*C. dirus*), which has become extinct. This latter species was relatively large, growing to about 2 m (6½ ft) in length, and of a heavier build than contemporary wolves.

A reinvasion of North America saw the grey wolf (*Canis lupus*) returning to the continent where wild canids evolved. This is the form sometimes known as the Canadian timber wolf, often occurring in forested areas.

Knowledge about the dire wolf has been greatly assisted by the discovery of the bodies of over 2000 of these canids at the site of the tar pits of Rancho La Brea, close to the present-day city of Los Angeles. Starting about 40,000 years ago, oil began to bubble up to the surface at this site, and as some components vaporized, sticky deposits of tar were left behind. When this was covered with water, it created the impression of drinking pools. Animals were attracted here as a consequence, and then became stuck fast in the tar, gradually sinking into the morass.

Herbivores trapped in these pools drew the attention of scavengers such as dire wolves, who then suffered a similar fate. Other species, which were active hunters, generally avoided being enticed into the tar pits, so there seems little doubt that dire wolves had a similar role to *Osteoborus*, and were primarily scavengers, seeking out carrion and using their powerful jaws to crush bones when they came across a suitable carcass.

No convincing evidence exists to suggest that canids had developed any form of social structure for hunting purposes up until the Pleistocene epoch. Study of the skull structure has led to the suggestion that the prorean gyrus, part of the frontal lobe of the brain, is enlarged in social canids. This change first starts to become apparent from *Leptocyon* onwards, and has become clearly apparent in contemporary canids, such as grey wolves. It is absent in foxes, which do not display this degree of social organization.

Our fossil knowledge of canids is far from complete, and there are some tantalizing indicators that some other species successfully crossed the Bering land bridge, although they subsequently failed to establish themselves in North America. Remains of *Cuon* species, for example, have been found here in localities as far apart as Alaska and Mexico, although this genus is no longer represented here. Similarly, jackals may have occurred in North America for a period as well.

It was probably also at the start of the Pleistocene that canids began to move southwards and reached South America, although there are significant gaps in the fossil record for this process of colonization. In fact, the earliest evidence to date of canids here has been unearthed close to the Atlantic coast in Buenos Aires province, Argentina. This is a considerable distance southwards from the Panamanian land bridge linking the northern and southern American continents and it is possible that canids first entered South America at an earlier stage, during the preceding Pliocene epoch, for example.

The increase in the areas of grassland probably facilitated this process. Among the early invaders about 2 million years ago was *Cerdocyon* whose descendants still inhabit this continent. But the influx of canids and subsequent specialization apparent in species such as the maned wolf (*Chrysocyon brachyurus*) suggests that development did not occur in the northern part of the continent. Fossil evidence suggests instead that having moved south, the canids then radiated from the vicinity of the highlands of Brazil. This is still where the greatest number of species can be found. Suitable habitat further north, in the Guianan highlands, for example, is not occupied by such a divergence of species, as could be expected if they had simply moved southwards. In fact, two monotypic genera – *Lycalopex* (now reclassified as *Dusicyon vetulus*) and *Chrysocyon* – are both endemic to this part of Brazil, indicating that they evolved here.

The evolution of the maned wolf (*Chrysocyon branchyurus*) in South America remains a mystery at present.

The grey fox (*Urocyon cinereoargenteus*) is the only wild canid whose current range includes both North and South America.

During the Pleistocene, part of the region in the east was arid and it is known that the extent of the Amazon forest fluctuated. This variation in habitat presumably contributed to the selection pressures on the different species, resulting in increasing diversity within the group.

Changes at the end of this epoch nevertheless saw the demise of several genera which had been present in South America. *Protocyon*, the oldest genus unearthed here, as well as *Theriodictis* both died out, while *Canis* species withdrew to more northerly parts of the Americas. Today, the coyote (*Canis latrans*) is the most southerly distributed member of this genus, extending only into northern Central America.

The grey fox (*Urocyon cinereoargenteus*) is now the only species which is found on both continents, and its range in South America is very limited – to just beyond the point where Central America merges into it. The remaining nine species are confined exclusively to the southern land mass, which is a further indication that they evolved here, rather than spreading from the north.

AUSTRALIA

Australia is unique among the inhabited continents in having no indigenous wild dogs. This is an accident of history, as far as can be ascertained, although fossil evidence about Australia's early mammalian fauna is remarkably sparse. Whereas the first mammals have been traced back over 200 million years in Europe, to the Triassic, the oldest mammalian fossils unearthed on the Australian continent date back just over 23 million years.

There have been some tantalizing clues that older fossils may await discovery here, however, most notably in the form of fossil fleas dating from the late Cretaceous era. A study of their mouthparts suggests they were actually mammalian parasites.

Mammals also existed in Antarctica, before it became a frozen wasteland, at least 45 million years ago, at a time when Antarctica and Australia were still joined as part of the ancient southern continent called Gondwanaland. The final bridge between these land masses was severed as recently as 37 million years ago. After this, Australia's mammalian population evolved in isolation. No protocanid group had reached here by this stage.

Then, about 15 million years ago, Australia's northward drift brought it closer to the Indonesian area of south-eastern Asia. This led to the formation of New Guinea and opened the way for groups of mammals to cross from Asia into Australia for the first time. Among the earliest invaders, assisted by their power of flight, were the bats, but no canids completed this journey.

A much later, yet highly significant colonization of Australia then occurred just 50,000 years ago, when the first human settlers reached the continent. The Aborigines probably came from New Guinea, or possibly further north in Asia. They brought with them the first and only canid which has established itself in Australia – the dingo (*Canis familiaris dingo*).

The precise date of the introduction of the dingo is unclear, but it occurred after the domestication of the dog began, some 12,000 years ago. Today, dogs which are similar to the dingo in appearance can be found living a semi-feral existence with tribes in New Guinea. In recent years, they have attracted attention from dog owners elsewhere in the world. They are known as New

Guinea singing dogs, because of the musical sounds of their vocalizations, but they cannot be considered fully domesticated. Indeed, they are perhaps most frequently encountered in zoological collections at present, rather than as household pets.

Other localized indigenous dogs with a similar feral lifestyle from this area include the New Ireland dog and the Papuan dog, both of which could have contributed to the ancestry of the dingo, although there are anatomical differences between them.

Estimates suggest that dingoes arrived in Australia between 4000 and 8000 years ago. Certainly, the dingo has changed little in its appearance over the past 3000 years, as comparisons of skeletal material have confirmed. But there is no evidence to suggest that it occurred in its present form on New Guinea. Indeed, the earliest evidence of the existence of dogs here dates back just 1500 years, which is well after the likely introduction of the dingo to Australia. This does not, of course, eliminate the possibility: it may simply be that their remains have yet to be discovered.

Another strange aspect to the dingo's appearance in Australia is that, contrary to popular belief, it does not have a close relationship with the Aborigines. Indeed it has proved to be virtually impossible to domesticate and train. Even experienced and sympathetic dog trainers have failed to instil

The origins of the New Guinea singing dog are unclear, but it would seem to be related to the dingo, which it resembles in appearance. These dogs are kept in a semi-domesticated state on New Guinea itself.

obedience into dingoes, nor is there any evidence to show that the Aborigines have ever done so, in terms of utilizing dingoes for hunting purposes.

Even in their rock art, Aborigines portray dingoes as rather remote associates, rather than as companions.

Studies of Aboriginal communities have revealed that these dogs tend to be scavengers, rather like the red fox in European cities today. Dingoes have become somewhat bolder, however, allowing themselves to be petted by the Aborigines for periods, but they are not normally fed. At night, when the desert temperatures plummet down close to zero, man and dog then huddle together to keep warm, for mutual benefit.

The lack of dependence on the dingo by the Aborigines suggests that their introduction to Australia may have been fortuitous, rather than an essential part of the early migratory wave of people settling here. As an opportunist, the dingo would have hunted kangaroos, and then as the era of white colonization began, they turned to sheep as a source of food. At this stage, they also encountered domestic dogs for the first time.

Cross-breeding between dingoes and domestic dogs has occurred regularly. In fact, a partial dingo ancestry is claimed for various Australian breeds of dog, notably the Australian cattle dog, which was evolved during the 1800s. While the dingo itself was found to be too unruly to be a working dog, it possessed considerable stamina and powers of endurance. These were vital qualities for dogs expected to work in the hot and often inhospitable terrain of Australia. Dingoes also reputedly imparted another characteristic to this breed – the ability to work silently, thus avoiding any panic in the herd.

THE DOMESTICATION PROCESS

It seems likely that the domestication of the dog did not occur in just one place at a single time. What is clear is that all of the 350 or so breeds in the world today are descended from the grey wolf (*Canis lupus*), ranging from the tiny chihuahua, standing just a few centimetres tall at the shoulder, up to the giant Irish wolfhound, which measures over a metre in height.

This great diversity in size and appearance has occurred within a relatively small number of generations, although it is a reflection of human selective pressure. The origins of this unique alliance between people and dogs dates back at least 12,000 years.

Wolf packs would have been well-known to the tribes of this era. It is quite likely that young wolves would have been adopted into communities from time to time, perhaps as orphans. In turn, they may have bred, and so the resulting cubs would have become used to human company.

At this stage, towards the end of the last Ice Age, the frozen tundra areas of the north were being replaced by forests. In this changing environment, it would have been helpful for hunters to have the dogs' scenting skills, in order to locate quarry. The dogs themselves would then have been rewarded with food.

The range of size within domestic breeds is not especially surprising, when set against the variance of size noted in the grey wolf through its range. Four distinct races of wolves are thought to have contributed to the ancestry of contemporary breeds. These range in size from Asiatic wolves which may

The head shape and coat length are two features which have been affected by domestication, as is evident by comparing a grey wolf (*Canis lupus*) with a domestic dog (*Canis familiaris*) – in this case a boxer (below). The domestication process is thought to have begun about 12,000 years ago.

weigh as little as 12 kg (27 lb) up to the largest of the North American wolves, which can be as heavy as 80 kg (177 lb).

Selective breeding began quite early during the domestication process. About 9000 years ago, there was already a noticeable divergence in the size of dogs. Archaelogical remains unearthed in the Beaverhead Mountain area of Idaho, USA, have revealed both a small dog, equivalent in size to a contemporary beagle, and a significantly larger, retriever-like dog. It has been estimated that only about 20 mutations would need to have occurred, in the 4000 or so generations of domestic dog, to explain the wide variance in appearance of today's breeds. These would have affected body size and physical traits, as well as the coat.

It is interesting that some breeds have remained similar in appearance to their lupine ancestors. Significantly, these tend to be the breeds developed in the far north, and are generally characterized as the spitz breeds. They are used for hunting and guarding purposes, as well as pulling sledges, and so fulfil a similar role to their ancestors.

Other groups of dogs have been subjected to much greater selective pressures, which helps to explain why their appearance and size has been altered so dramatically. Nowhere is this more evident than in the toy breeds, which have been developed over recent centuries as companion dogs. Yet even in this category, there are still breeds, albeit dramatically scaled down in size, that bear an unmistakable similarity in appearance to the grey wolf. The Keeshond, evolved in the Netherlands as a barge dog, is a typical example. Although its coat is rather more profuse, it still retains a distinctive wolf grey coloration.

Within the toy group, however, there has been a tendency to encourage white coloration among the more lupine members, as seen in the Japanese spitz, a diminutive breed averaging around 33 cm (13 in) at the shoulder, and weighing about 5 kg (11 lb).

Anatomical features have been dramatically modified through selective breeding from the original wolf stock. This has led to the emergence of more specialized working breeds, and is particularly evident in the hound group. Whereas wolves hunt using a combination of eyesight and scenting skill, many domestic breeds of hound can be divided into either scent hounds or sight hounds.

The scent hounds, such as the bloodhound, rely almost exclusively on their tracking skills to locate their quarry. Their nose and nasal chambers are relatively large, in order to maximize the ability to detect scents. In contrast, breeds such as the greyhound – the sight hound category – have a much narrower nose and more forward directed eyes. Their keen eyesight enables them to locate and pursue game depending primarily on this sense. For this purpose, their eyes tend to be directed forwards, whereas in wolves they are positioned more on the side of the head.

While the grey wolf itself has declined in recent years in the face of increasing urbanization, particularly in Europe, its descendant, in the form of the domestic dog continues, as a result of its co-operative lifestyle with people, to spread much further afield to all continents.

Dogs have adapted to new habitats and tasks under human patronage. In Europe today, where the grey wolf population is comprised of just a few thousand individuals, the number of domestic dogs is approaching 30 million. This is indisputable evidence of the way in which the canine evolutionary process has been shaped over recent millennia by human intervention, and the dramatic impact of this process in social terms.

EVOLUTIONARY ANALYSIS

While the physical characteristics of an animal can change quite rapidly, as the diversity present within the domestic dog population has confirmed, there are other underlying features which tend to be more stable, and thus are of greater value both for taxonomic purposes and for unravelling the relationship between members of the family Canidae.

The pattern of dentition is one obvious characteristic that has been used for this purpose. The traditional view was that there were three subfamilies within the Canidae, with most species being grouped in the subfamily Caninae. The wild dogs in the second subfamily, Simocyoninae, were grouped on the basis that the first molar tooth in their lower jaw was significantly smaller than in the Caninae. Furthermore, there was no depression towards the rear of the tooth, and only a very small inner cusp here. These dental characteristics applied to three species – the African hunting dog (*Lycaon pictus*); the dhole (*Cuon alpinus*) and the bush dog (*Speothos venaticus*). The so-called trenchant feature of this tooth is an ancient one in members of family Canidae, and can be traced back in fossils to the Oligocene era.

But a comparison of these three species reveals that they have no other obvious features which would justify placing them in a subfamily on their own. Indeed, there are a number of anatomically significant differences, not the least of which is the fact that only the dhole and the bush dog have a reduction in the overall number of teeth, but here there is no consistency. Bush dogs have only 38 teeth, while the dhole possesses 40, and, in common with the majority of the Canidae, the African hunting dog has 42 in total.

Meanwhile, research has shown that in the case of the African hunting dog, the trenchant first lower molar is not apparent in all ancestral forms, but is actually a relatively modern evolutionary development.

The teeth are used as the distinguishing feature of the third subfamily as well. In this case however, it is the number of teeth, rather than their structure which was deemed to be significant. The bat-eared fox (*Otocyon megalotis*) is grouped on its own, in the subfamily Otocyoninae, since it has more teeth than any other species.

Rather than relying on gross anatomical features to unravel the relationship between the various species, in recent years the emphasis has shifted to cytogenetic studies. This began during the 1920s, with attempts to map the number of diploid (paired) chromosomes of each species. Chromosomes are located in the nucleus of each living cell, and carry the genetic material in the form of DNA (deoxyribonucleic acid).

The DNA itself is in the form of a double helix structure. This is comprised of a sequence of bases, linked to sugars and phosphates within the DNA molecule. The DNA sequences at the core of the genetic process are unique. It is now possible to study DNA of different species, and, by seeking out

93

similarities, not only assess current relationships but also calculate the stage at which in the past the species may have separated.

Unfortunately, the historical value of this technique in the case of the Canidae has proved somewhat limited to date, since it appears that the major divergence of today's species only occurred quite recently in evolutionary terms – about 10 million years ago. However, the technique has suggested two distinct lineages, separating the *Vulpes* species from the wolf-like canids.

A test which has given further insight into the canid evolutionary process examines genetic differences between species based on a technique called protein electrophoresis. The results have been in broad accord with the DNA work that has been carried out, and challenge some of the established views concerning relationships within the Canidae. Not all species have yet been studied (notably some of the South American foxes), but using these laboratory-based methods, it would appear that there are six distinct groups within the Canidae.

The grey wolf (*Canis lupus*) and domestic dog (*C. familiaris*) show the closest relationship within the lupine lineage, as expected. The coyote (*C. latrans*), having evolved around 2 million years ago, is somewhat distant from them in evolutionary terms. The black-backed jackal (*C. mesomelas*) which also first appeared about this time in Africa appears to share its ancestry with the bush dog (*Speothos venaticus*).

Another member of the former subfamily Simocyoninae, the African wild dog (*Lycaon pictus*) is also now grouped in this lupine category. Its fossil history is consistent with its new taxonomic position, since ancestral forms of *Lycaon* have been unearthed in Europe, and it now appears that these were descended from lupine stock.

The first divergence within this group appears to have taken place some 6 million years ago, when the black-backed jackal and bush dog split off from the ancestral line, the latter being the only wolf-like canid represented in South America.

The other canids which have been studied from this part of the world appear to divide into two separate groups. It seems that the small foxes diverged from ancestral stock between 3 and 6 million years ago, with the maned wolf (*Chrysocyon brachyurus*) and the bush dog being of an older lineage. Unfortunately, there is a shortage of fossilized evidence in the case of the South American canids. The earliest remains of the maned wolf unearthed so far only date back as far as the mid-Pleistocene, but the figures that have been obtained by laboratory means from the study of living canids appear to correspond quite well with the available data from fossilized remains.

The vulpine foxes date back in the fossil record to the mid-Miocene, around 10 million years ago. While it may appear that the Arctic (*Alopex lagopus*) and swift (*Vulpes velox*) foxes do not share a close common ancestry, this view is not borne out by a study of their chromosomes. In fact, they share a unique karyotype not encountered in any other member of the entire family. They also show a clear similarity to the red fox (*Vulpes vulpes*).

Studies suggest that the red fox actually began to diverge from the Cape fox (*Vulpes chama*) about 5 million years ago, although at present, there is no fossilized evidence to support this contention, with the earliest available records being some 4 million years later. This type of analysis is therefore not only useful in detecting relationships, it can also help to fill in potential gaps which exist in the fossil record, although obviously, firm proof is desirable for accurate mapping of the evolutionary pathway.

Tests have revealed that there are three species within the Canidae which stand apart. The previous separation of the bat-eared fox would appear valid, on karyotypic as well as morphological grounds. It dates back in the fossil record about 3 million years, but is almost certainly of older lineage.

The grey fox (*Urocyon cinereoargenteus*) has also not diverged from canid stock in recent times. It evolved in the late Miocene, around 9 million years ago, and has since been the ancestor of the island grey fox (*Urocyon littoralis*).

Studies have shown that the raccoon dog (*Nyctereutes procyonoides*) also bears no close relationship with other members of the family. It has not appeared in the fossil record in North America, and it would seem to have played no part in the ancestry of the bush dog, as some authors have suggested.

These laboratory techniques are helping to revolutionize the science of taxonomy, and are an invaluable aid in assessing evolutionary theories, in a way that has not been possible previously. They can also provide specific clues as to which part of the geological record is most likely to reveal crucial missing evidence about the evolution of canids. It seems likely that this means of piecing together the fossil history of the family will become increasingly important over the years ahead.

Chapter 5
The Canid Family

The taxonomy used throughout this book is based on that adopted by the IUCN/SSC Canid and Wolf Specialist Groups, as part of the Canid Action Plan, which is intended to safeguard the future of all wild canids on the planet. The 34 living species are listed in the family Canidae, with the majority of species being classified in just three genera.

Wolves and jackals form the genus *Canis* (along with the dingo and domestic dog), while most of the South American foxes, described as 'zorros' after the Spanish word for 'fox', are grouped in the genus *Dusicyon* – the crab-eating zorro is listed separately on its own in the genus *Cerdocyon*. Foxes occurring in the Old World are largely classified in the genus *Vulpes*, along with the North American species, the swift fox (*V. velox*).

Taxonomy is not a static science, however, as mentioned previously (see page 95), and it is undergoing radical changes in some areas because of genetic studies. Formerly, taxonomists were forced to rely simply on morphological traits when assessing relationships between species, but this situation is continuing to change as these new techniques are utilized.

In broad terms, there is relatively little controversy about the taxonomy of the Canidae, although the relationships of the zorros, which are the least-studied members of the family, have been the subject of past debate. More detailed study over the past decade has led to broad agreement that the fennec fox (*Fennecus zerda*) is best grouped in a genus on its own, rather than as a member of the genus *Vulpes*. Similarly, the North American grey foxes have been removed from this genus, and accorded individual recognition in the genus *Urocyon*.

Unravelling the validity of subspecific claims is a much more complex task, although nevertheless, it is very important. Subspecies, representing distinctive, individual populations and having a range which is likely to be considerably more restricted than that of the species itself, represent the most basic unit in the classificatory tree. If attempts at conservation are to be successful, this is the level at which they must be judged, although because of the attendant complexities, efforts tend to be concentrated more towards the overall needs of the species.

The classificatory system operates through a series of ranks, right down to individual subspecies, as shown by the example below, involving the bush dog:

Order:	Mammalia
Family:	Canidae
Genus:	*Speothos*
Species:	*Speothos venaticus*
Subspecies:	*S. venaticus venaticus*
	S. venaticus wingei

The first subspecies to be described, known as the nominate species, can be recognized by the repetition of the specific epithet, in this case '*venaticus*'. *S. venaticus* itself was first described in the scientific literature in 1839, while *S.v.wingei* was written up some years later in 1911.

However, as in many other groups of animals, the taxonomy of the Canidae, is not clear-cut and confusion can still arise, particularly over the classification of the South American canids. In older works you will often find species described that are no longer required as separate species today. For example, there is the case of Darwin's fox (*Dusicyon fulvipes*), sometimes described as the Chiloe fox, after the island off the coast of Chile where Charles Darwin originally found it during his round-the-world voyage on HMS *Beagle*. Darwin had gone ashore with a surveying party, and observed the fox watching them. He was able to approach the unfortunate creature and kill it with a blow from his geological hammer. On his return to England, the fox was mounted and displayed in the museum of the Zoological Society.

In colour, Darwin's fox is identical to the culpeo (*Dusicyon griseus*), but it is somewhat smaller in size. Nowadays it is generally accepted that it is simply an island form of the mainland species, rather than a species in its own right. However, recently, in 1990, individuals living on the mainland corresponding more closely in appearance to Darwin's fox have been reported for the first time. This discovery opens up this particular taxonomic area again, suggesting that there could now be a stronger case for separating Darwin's fox and the culpeo if distinct populations are occurring in the same area. Further study, based on genetics, will be needed to resolve the debate.

Another similar case concerns the so-called Peruvian fox (*Dusicyon inca*). This species is apparently known from just a single specimen, obtained at an altitude of about 4000 m (13,000 ft). It resembles Azara's zorro (*Dusicyon gymnocercus*) in colour, although it is less colourful, with a greyer tinge to its back and tawny instead of reddish markings elsewhere. Their range is widely separated, however, with Azara's zorro occurring in a far more south-easterly location (see page 178) than the supposed Peruvian fox. This latter form is now thought to be most closely allied to the culpeo (*Dusicyon culpaeus*), which ranges into this region, although the precise distribution of various wild canids on this continent is still not clearly defined.

A third instance of taxonomic confusion surrounds the Santa Elena fox (*Dusicyon culpaeolus*), recorded to date from a small area in the south-east of Uruguay. Here it is separated from the current distribution of the culpeo, whose nearest population occurs further to the west in Argentina. Although smaller than the culpeo, the Santa Elena fox has similar coloration and markings, which distinguishes it from the predominantly grey members of the genus. It appears that the Santa Elena fox may represent a relic population of the culpeo which has become isolated, possibly by climatic changes since the end of the last Ice Age. The culpeo's ancestors used to occur right across the Argentine pampas, into what is present-day Uruguay. Today, however, the Santa Elena fox represents the only living evidence of this former distribution.

Thought to be confined just to the departments of Rio Negro and Soriano in Uruguay, the Santa Elena fox cannot as yet be considered sufficiently diverse to be a separate species. Instead, it has been classified as a subspecies of the culpeo called *Dusicyon culpaeus culpaeolus*. Nothing is known about the population size of these foxes, but the paucity of specimens (with just one in the British Museum collection) suggests that they are rare.

In the following chapters, the arrangement of the species is based broadly upon their geographical distribution, following the system adopted in the IUCN/SSC Action Plan. The wide range of some species, notably the red fox (*Vulpes vulpes*), means that a strict continental approach is not possible; this canid, for example, is now found on all continents apart from South America, following its introduction to Australia during the last century. Mention is also made of the Falkland Island wolf (*Dusicyon australis*), which is the only species of canid to have become extinct in recent times.

Chapter 6
Canids of the Holarctic

Some wolves and foxes have a distribution that is basically circumpolar, extending through North America, and northern parts of Europe and Asia. This is essentially the result of past differences in the links between continents, notably the existence of the Bering land bridge (see page 85), which enabled species to move freely between North America and Eurasia, up until the end of the last Ice Age.

There is also evidence that the ice sheets in this region have permitted species to spread more widely than would otherwise have been possible in a more temperate zone. They almost certainly enabled the Arctic fox (*Alopex lagopus*) to reach Iceland, for example, which was formed directly out of sea bed by volcanic activity some 20 million years ago, rather than being attached to an existing land mass. This species is the largest carnivore and the only wild canid to have colonized the island.

Arctic fox *Alopex lagopus*

DISTRIBUTION
Circumpolar, ranging into the tundra and Arctic areas of Eurasia, North America and islands including Iceland, Greenland and Spitzbergen. There is also a population in the Altai Mountains, in Central Asia.

The Arctic fox is the only canid that has successfully adapted to life in the far north, outside the temperate region, and achieved a circumpolar distribution. Males tend to be about 0.5 kg (1 lb) heavier than females, averaging around 3.5 kg (7.7 lb). Their small ears and short legs contrast with their long bushy tail which is equivalent to more than half their head and body length combined, measuring approximately 30 cm (12 in). This may serve as an important means of communication between individuals, allowing the reduction in the size of their ears, which restricts heat loss from their bodies.

Other adaptations to the climate have been made. The soles of the feet of the Arctic fox are entirely covered with hair, protecting them from frostbite as they walk on frozen ground. This has given rise to the scientific name 'lagopus', which means 'hare-footed'. The fur covering the body is thick, and two distinct colour forms are known: the dominant blue form and the recessive white variant.

There are marked variations in the proportions of the two forms within the species' range. Blue Arctic foxes are most numerous towards the edges of their distribution. They generally constitute less than 1 per cent of the overall population, but show a marked increase in some areas such as western Alaska and on islands such as the Pribiloff group. In the neighbourhood of Thule in Greenland, blue-phase foxes constitute nearly 90 per cent of the population.

Two main factors appear to influence the proportions of the colour forms. It is noticeable that where lemmings (*Lemmus* spp.) occur, the proportion of white-coated Arctic foxes is relatively high, whereas the blue variety tends to dominate in other areas. Human influence also has a bearing on the relative numbers of these colours within some populations. This is particularly evident on islands such as the Pribiloffs. Here trappers have deliberately removed the white form, to increase the numbers of the more valuable blue form within the island population.

Both colour morphs undergo a seasonal change in appearance, beginning in the autumn. The dense new winter coat typically starts to appear on the belly first, spreading on to the flanks and finally the back. Its insulation value is higher than that of any other mammal. The white form turns pure white at this stage, giving maximal camouflage against a snowy landscape, while the blue form turns a light shade of blue, bordering on pale grey.

In the spring, they moult again, shedding the dense underfur with its high insulation value. White foxes at this stage become brownish-grey, paler on the underparts, while the blue colour variant is transformed into a dark chocolate-brown shade.

It is clear that in the past Arctic foxes ranged over a much wider area than they do today. Their remains have been found in many European countries, including France, Britain, Germany, Poland and Switzerland. This indicates that the species may well have roamed throughout Europe at some stage, and is now reduced to the northern edges of its former range in this part of the world.

Few wild canids are as bold as the Arctic fox, and as fearless of people. Even today, after centuries of persecution, these foxes may approach closely,

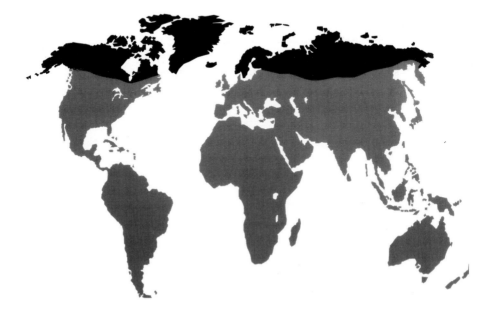

Distribution of the Arctic fox (*Alopex lagopus*).

The bleak, treeless terrain of the far north is home to the Arctic fox (*Alopex lagopus*). This is a view of Iceland, where the species is heavily hunted.

displaying a natural inquisitiveness. When a party of explorers was wrecked on Bering Island in 1741, they described how the Arctic foxes stole food, and came so close that they directly interfered with the skinning of seals, rather like unruly domestic dogs.

Relatively little is known about the movements of Arctic foxes, however, although it is known that they can travel considerable distances. They have been observed as far as 640 km (397 miles) north of the Alaskan coast, on sea ice, and tagging has confirmed that animals from the former USSR have crossed to Alaska. It is clear that some individuals travel huge distances during their lives, being trapped as far as 1500 km (931 miles) from where they were originally marked. It is thought that some foxes are even carried to other areas on drifting floes as sea ice melts in the spring.

Distinct seasonal movements have been recorded in Alaska, with the foxes moving northwards as the ice extends in the autumn, depending on the availability of food. They then return to inland areas to mate in late winter, staying here through until the autumn.

As may be expected, Arctic foxes are opportunistic in their feeding habits, although rodents, particularly lemmings, feature prominently in their diet. The decline in the wolf population has affected Arctic foxes, since they used to scavenge from wolf kills, being unable to overcome large animals themselves.

Fish and other marine creatures will be eaten readily, as well as carrion. On occasions, Arctic foxes may be cannibalistic. Those living close to the coast will hunt sea birds such as little auks (*Plautus alle*). Where food is plentiful, a number of these foxes may be seen; 40 were observed feeding together on the body of a dead walrus (*Odobenus rosmarus*) which had been frozen in sea ice.

They had dug down through 0.6 m (2 ft) of ice, and gnawed their way into the carcass. Vegetation, including grasses and even seaweed, may also be consumed, especially when other food is in short supply.

Not surprisingly, Arctic foxes may store food when it is plentiful, returning later to feed on it, at least in some part of their range. Caching is most likely to occur just after the snow has melted in the springtime. At this time of year, it becomes easier for foxes to catch rodents, which are forced out of their burrows by flooding. Caches are sited in well-concealed localities, away from pups.

The significance of rodents in the diet of Arctic foxes is shown by an examination of their respective population cycles. In the vicinity of Barrow, Alaska, where the relationship between the Arctic fox and the brown lemming (*Lemmus trimucronatus*) has been studied for more than 30 years, it has been found that both populations exhibit a 4-year cycle, with the highest fox numbers coinciding with, or occurring just after a peak in the population of the lemming.

Litter size can also be correlated with the availability of lemmings, according to research carried out in Canada. It declines dramatically as the lemming population collapses. Both sexes of Arctic fox mature at about 10 months old, with the mating season lasting from February to May. They appear to be monogamous in the wild, with a pair spending much of their time together throughout the breeding period.

The female will give birth to her litter in an underground den, after a gestation period lasting 52 days. These dens are often large, and may be used repeatedly over many years. One estimate suggests that some dens may be occupied for more than three centuries, by successive generations of foxes, but this is likely to be exceptional.

The type of terrain determines the structure of the den itself. Low mounds, up to 4 m (13 ft) in height are favoured in the north Alaskan tundra. Here, only the upper part of the ground thaws out, the underlying permafrost actually preventing successful excavation of a burrow.

The presence of fox dens has a dramatic impact on the local landscape, stimulating the growth of vegetation which is clearly noticeable in the summer. The addition of nutrients to the soil, and the breaking up of the soil help to encourage this change. In other areas, however, foxes may be unable to tunnel because the soil may be too sandy and loose, causing it to collapse readily, and they may choose to make their dens amongst rocks.

Most dens have more than one entrance. Four would appear to be the average number, but at one site in northern Alaska, 26 entrances were associated with a large den which occupied an area in excess of 100 m^2 (1076 ft^2) – about three times the average size.

The density of dens is quite variable, and is presumably influenced to some extent by the availability of food. In suitable areas, typically along river banks, there may be more than two dens per square kilometre ($\frac{1}{2}$ square mile). In island situations, dens may be closer together, although the number of pups reared tends to be correspondingly lower than elsewhere.

Little is known about the territoriality of these foxes. Observations in Iceland reveal that their home range can extend from 8.6 to 18.5 km^2 (3–7 square miles), and there is little overlap in these areas.

In the autumn, berries may help to provide nourishment for Arctic foxes.

Some pairs may occupy a territory for up to 5 years. In Iceland, the average litter size is just over five, whereas in Canada, this figure is effectively doubled. Fecundity is influenced by diet, with foxes in coastal areas tending to be far less prolific than those living elsewhere. When rodents are plentiful, litter size increases accordingly, with up to 19 pups being born in a single litter.

Young Arctic foxes weigh about 56 g (2 oz) at birth, and have a body covering of short brown fur, which has a velvety texture. The male assists in the rearing of his offspring, and in some areas, notably Iceland, females from the previous year which are not breeding may stay as part of a family group, acting as helpers. They remain at the den for up to 2 months after the birth of the cubs, before dispersing further afield, and will probably have a litter themselves in the following year.

The cubs will first emerge from the den when they are 3 weeks old, but it will be perhaps another 8 weeks before they start to accompany their parents on hunting trips. Ultimately, the male will leave the group first, with the litter remaining together for up to 6 months, dispersing in the autumn, or after the winter period, according to recent radiotracking studies. They frequently travel a considerable distance at this stage – up to 2000 km (1240 miles).

A number of predators threaten Arctic foxes, and possibly for this reason, they tend to be nocturnal, even during the summer period, when the far north is subject to almost constant light. Birds of prey, including snowy owls (*Nyctea scandiaca*) and golden eagles (*Aquila chrysaetos*) will take them, given the opportunity, but their winter coat provides an effective camouflage against these birds on a snowy background.

On the ground, polar bears (*Ursus maritimus*), wolverines (*Gulo gulo*) and even red foxes (*Vulpes vulpes*) may also kill Arctic foxes, while in terms of disease, rabies occurs in various areas of their range, and can result in widespread local mortality. This infection is apparently most common during the colder months of the year. Trapping for their fur is significant in some areas such as Iceland, but does not appear to have impacted seriously on the population as a whole.

Overall, the status of the Arctic fox gives no cause for concern, although one very localized subspecies – *Alopex lagopus semenovi* – is on the verge of extinction. Confined to Mednij Island, part of the Commander Group on the north-eastern coast of the former USSR, they were trapped annually for their fur in large numbers from 1920 up until 1950. Trapping finally ceased during 1965, but then a drastic decline in numbers began in 1972 as a result of mange, thought to have been introduced by domestic dogs which visit the island periodically with sailors.

By 1979 it was thought that the subspecies had disappeared, but further studies have revealed that up to 120 still occur on the island. It is hoped that the population will increase again, provided that dogs, which will also kill these foxes directly, can be kept off Mednij, and the remaining animals prove more resistant to mange.

Interaction with red foxes is thought to underlie the decline of the Arctic fox in Scandinavia. The red fox will drive out its smaller relative, and take over its territory. In spite of protective measures in force in Sweden for more than 50 years, the Arctic fox does not appear to have undergone any significant recovery in numbers here.

Coyote (prairie wolf; brush wolf) *Canis latrans*

DISTRIBUTION
Occurs in Alaska and throughout southern-central areas of Canada, across the entire USA extending via Mexico into the northern part of Central America.

The name 'coyote' is a derivation of the ancient Aztec word '*coyotl*', which means 'barking dog', and describes the calls of these canids. Averaging around 50 cm (19 in) high at the shoulders, coyotes weigh up to 16 kg (35 lb). Black ticking is apparent on their coats, with the tip of the tail being solid black in colour. The underparts are pale, bordering on white in some cases.

Coyotes evolved as animals of the plains, originally inhabiting grass and areas on the western side of North America. They occupied parts of the country where they did not come into contact with grey wolves, which competed more successfully in such regions. The decline of both the grey (*C. lupus*) and the red (*C. rufus*) wolf has enabled a significant expansion of the coyote's range during the present century. The species now enjoys the widest natural range of latitude of any terrestrial mammal.

Their opportunistic nature is a major reason underlying their success. Coyotes will take a wide variety of mammalian species, as well as many reptiles, amphibians, fish and invertebrates. Although they prefer to feed on freshly caught creatures, they will also consume carrion when necessary. Fruit also features prominently in their diet, according to the season. Even grass may be eaten during the winter, when other foods are scarce.

Distribution of the coyote (*Canis latrans*).

Coyotes have long been persecuted by farmers because of attacks on domestic livestock. Newborn animals are especially at risk although even adult cattle, for example, may fall victim to coyotes if these canids are working together in a group. Unlike wolves, however, coyotes do not regularly associate in packs. Occasionally, single-sex parties may be observed, comprising up to six individuals, but these usually break up readily.

Pairing takes place in January and February, when the female enters oestrus after a pro-oestrus period which may have lasted 3 months. At this stage, she may be courted by several males, with their pursuit having built up over 4 weeks. Ultimately, it is the female's choice as to a partner, and other males do not attempt to interfere with the mating process.

A pair may use a den either dug by themselves or taken over from other animals, such as skunks (*Mephitis* spp.), and return to this site regularly. The typical litter size is about six pups, but as many as 19 have been recorded. The young leave the nest almost as soon as their eyes are open, around 2 weeks of age. The male is largely responsible for providing food for the litter as well as his mate. Helpers may guard the offspring, but are not involved in caring for them directly.

Soon after leaving the den, the young coyotes start to attempt to catch insects. Gradually, the litter begins to disperse towards the end of their first year. Some may travel long distances at this stage, with one coyote being known to have journeyed about 200 km (125 miles) in a fortnight. Many youngsters die at this stage, often because of human persecution. Traps and

105

The coyote (*Canis latrans*) is the most widely distributed canid in North America, as wolves have declined in numbers. This species continues to expand in some areas here.

poison account for many coyotes each year, while others are shot. In some areas, this is the major cause of mortality.

Disease is another important factor in regulating coyote numbers. Puppies are very susceptible to distemper, and may acquire this viral infection from contact with domestic dogs. Rabies is also a serious threat, causing widespread mortality in some areas. Parasites, notably roundworms, can be acquired from the female, and a heavy build-up can be fatal in a young animal. More localized parasitic problems, such as hookworms can affect populations in some areas.

Sometimes a young coyote will be killed by an older individual. Pairs will defend their territory from incursions. In areas where they occur in packs, there is a distinct order of dominance, and usually only the dominant pair will breed. It is not known how long coyotes live in the wild, but in zoo surroundings, they can live for nearly 22 years. A maximum lifespan of about 15 years is probably attained by free-living coyotes.

There is a considerable range in size between coyotes from different parts of their distribution. The largest individuals, from northern and mountainous areas, can weigh as much as 34 kg (75 lb), while those from the deserts of Mexico average around 11.5 kg (25 lb). There is also a corresponding difference in coloration, with desert-dwelling coyotes being brownish-yellow, whereas those from upland areas tend to be darker.

In the past it was only the coyotes in the southern part of the species' range that used to hunt largely at night or during the early mornings, when the temperature was relatively cool. Elsewhere they were mainly diurnal. Nowadays, however, through most of their North American range, coyotes are more nocturnal because of human persecution.

Its reputation as a major killer of domestic livestock is probably largely unwarranted. In an extensive study of the coyote's feeding habits, an examination of the stomach contents of over 8000 animals revealed that lagomorphs were by far the most significant individual item in their diet. Carrion, followed by rodents were the other items of significance, confirming the benefits of coyotes in controlling the numbers of agricultural pests.

The remains of farmstock was present in the stomach contents of about 20 per cent of the coyotes. The majority of these remains were of goats and sheep. Other studies suggest that the peak time for sheep-killing by coyotes is in the post-lambing period, when the coyotes are also breeding, and their food requirements are increased. Even so, it appears that it is injured coyotes that are most likely to prey upon farmstock, because such animals are easier to catch than rabbits or rodents.

In some areas, trapping can actually exacerbate the extent of sheep-killing, simply because this increases the numbers of injured coyotes. An animal that escapes from a trap is often handicapped for the rest of its life. Coyotes appear to have remarkable powers of recovery, however, often adapting well to handicaps such as missing feet.

Under normal circumstances, coyotes are adept hunters, and usually work in pairs. One of the dogs will set off in pursuit of a black-tailed jack rabbit (*Lepus californicus*), for example, with the other then moving forward, cutting off the animal as it attempts to weave away. This tactic is repeated by the coyotes until the rabbit becomes exhausted, allowing them to catch up with it.

On several occasions, coyotes have also been observed lurking close to hunting badgers (*Taxidea taxus*). This association can yield dividends if the badger digs up a rodent, while conversely, badgers may take advantage of a rabbit driven to earth by a coyote. There appears to be no direct communication between the species in such cases, however, and no question of sharing the kill.

Grey wolf *Canis lupus*

DISTRIBUTION
Used to occur throughout North America, Europe and Asia, but range now significantly reduced, particularly in Europe.

The grey wolf is the largest of all wild canids, although its size varies noticeably through its range. The biggest wolves are found in the far north, where the males, which are invariably bigger than the females, can measure over 80 cm (31 in) high at the shoulder and can weigh 80 kg (176 lb). Their coloration is also variable and tends to correspond to the background colour of their habitat. Colours vary from creamy white through sandy and reddish shades to grey and black.

Despite years of persecution, the grey wolf still has one of the widest distributions of all mammals, occurring throughout the northern hemisphere, above 15°N latitude. Today, following the dramatic decline in its range during recent centuries, remaining populations tend to be confined to remote areas, away from major areas of human settlement. In some places, such as Alaska and Northwest Territories, however, their range remains intact, and healthy populations of grey wolves are found here.

Moving further south, the situation changes dramatically. In the northwest of the USA, the grey wolf is almost extinct, with a remnant population here of just 30 individuals. Further to the south, it is already extinct in the USA, while in Mexico, the outlook for the species is exceedingly bleak. Only occasional single wolves or pairs still occur in this area. Estimates suggest fewer than 10 survive.

The situation is even worse in Europe. The grey wolf became extinct in England about 1486 before being exterminated in Scotland about 1743 and finally from Ireland in 1770. It has also vanished from many other European countries. Relic populations can now be found in just 8 out of the 23 countries which are members of the Council of Europe.

In Scandinavia, persecution has meant that wolves are now almost extinct in both Norway and Sweden, with probably fewer than 100 left in Finland. This population has been reinforced by wolves moving across the border from the former USSR, while in the north of the country, intensive hunting has effectively eliminated them in an area where reindeer (*Rangifer tarandus*) are economically significant.

Across the border in the former USSR, however, the wolf population has actually grown somewhat, because of habitat changes since World War 2. Formerly, there were few wolves in the old coniferous forests, largely because prey was limited in such surroundings. Clearance of this forest, and its replacement by deciduous woodland has enabled elk (moose) (*Alces alces*) populations to flourish, leading to a recovery in wolf numbers in this area. Ultimately, some of these wolves then crossed into Scandinavia.

Distribution of the grey wolf (*Canis lupus*). The dark tone indicates present distribution; the mid-grey tone indicates former distribution.

Grey wolves (*Canis lupus*) are highly social canids, with an increasing pack size enabling them to hunt larger prey.

In southern Europe, wolves ranged over almost the entire Iberian peninsula in 1840, disappearing at first from the east of the region. The most dramatic decline has occurred since 1950, to the extent that the grey wolf is now confined essentially to areas in the north-west of Spain, and the eastern side of Portugal. Nevertheless, there appears to have been an encouraging recovery in numbers in northern Spain since the mid-1970s, with recent estimates suggesting that there are now at least 1500 wolves in the country.

The situation appears to be less positive in Portugal, where the wolf population is comprised of probably little more than 100 individuals, with the majority being located in the province of Tras os Montes. Almost certainly, there is a movement of wolves across the border here with Spain. In some parts of Portugal, notably the Alentijo and the Algarve, the species is extinct.

The range of the grey wolf in Italy has been dramatically reduced during the present century, with the major period of decline taking place between 1945 and 1970. By 1973, it was estimated that there were barely 100 left in the country, confined mainly to isolated mountainous pockets. Grey wolves had already died out in Sicily by 1950.

Since they were given protection in 1977, it appears that the numbers of wolves in Italy has started to increase again, albeit on a small scale. Studies carried out during the 1980s suggest that their population now comprises around 200 individuals. These are to be found in central and southern areas.

Further eastwards, in Greece, grey wolves remain more numerous, although there is a wide divergence in population estimates here. The most recent and detailed studies, based on field work, suggest that around 500 is a

109

likely figure. The wolf population is concentrated in the north of the country, on the borders of Bulgaria and Turkey, while there are other pockets elsewhere in the country.

Even so, it appears that the grey wolf is declining in Greece. Although wolves are still hunted, habitat changes and a shortage of ungulate prey are probably the most important factors contributing to this situation. In some areas of Greece, hunting of wolves is still actively encouraged, with bounties being paid for dead animals.

In the countries bordering Greece, there is little accurate information on the number of grey wolves. In Turkey, for example, there are no data at all; the species is thought to be in decline, but not currently in serious danger.

To the north-east, wolf populations tend to be healthier, with an estimated population of 50,000 animals in the Asiatic region of the former USSR and a further 20,000 in the European sector. Good numbers still survive in Poland as well.

The species' range through the Middle East is far more tenuous however. It is highly endangered in the Sinai region of Egypt, with only about 30 individuals still surviving here, and they are afforded no protection. The same applies in Jordan, as well as Syria, with perhaps just 200 wolves still left in each country.

The situation is little better in adjacent parts of southern Asia, where population data are available. In India, the grey wolf is supposedly protected, but this legislation is hard to enforce, and numbers are declining. They could be as low as 1000 individuals now.

It is significant that grey wolves remain numerous essentially in those parts of the world where they do not come into close contact and hence conflict with people. The human antagonism towards the wolf, which dates back to the dawn of history, remains widespread. Now with the advent of powerful firearms, as well as traps and poisons, so the balance has swung inexorably against the wolf.

The risk to people from wolves is exceedingly low. Leaving aside attacks by rabid animals, there is virtually no evidence of attacks by wolves on people over the past century. There is some evidence from Italy that unaccompanied young children may have been killed by wolves, but even so, the popular reputation of the wolf as an unrelenting killer of people is completely unjustified.

Yet this image remains one of the most powerful barriers to the conservation of the grey wolf. It manifests itself in public opposition to attempts to reintroduce wolves to suitable areas of former habitat, as well as a reluctance to impose penalties on wolf hunters.

So-called 'sport hunting', as practised in Mediterranean countries such as Italy, is the major cause of wolf mortality in these areas. Hunters out in search of wild boar (*Sus scrofa*), for example, are not averse to killing wolves, should an opportunity present itself, and the chances of detection under these circumstances are remote.

The natural prey of wolves varies through their wide range. In the far north, it tends to be moose, while further south, red deer (*Cervus elaphus*) are frequent quarry. As these prey species have been eliminated in various areas, so the numbers of wolves have subsequently declined. In the Bavarian Forest

Grey wolves (*Canis lupus*) may occur in a variety of terrains, including wooded areas, through their wide range.

of Germany, for example, the wolf became extinct approximately 40 years after the last red deer were killed.

Elsewhere, the disappearance of natural prey species may force wolves into killing increasing numbers of farmstock, leading to even more conflict with people as a consequence. This in turn speeds their decline. In fact, there are now various parts of Europe where large wild ungulates are again reasonably common, but wolves have not recolonized many of these regions, probably because of the presence of humans.

Farmers often do not realize that in their defence of their livestock they are provoking further killing. Under normal circumstances, a wolf will eat its fill perhaps over the course of several days. But if it is being constantly harried, then it will tend to kill more frequently, eating what it can from the carcass, before moving on again to escape those pursuing it.

Sheep are most likely to fall prey to wolves in southern Europe. In Spain alone, it has been estimated that livestock losses resulting from attacks by wolves total about a million US dollars, with a quarter of this figure being paid in compensation. Surplus killing, induced by the sheer panic of a flock of sheep confined with a wolf in their midst, is significant in some areas. In central Italy, up to 100 sheep may be killed by a pack in a single night, although 10 or so is a more usual figure under such circumstances.

Contact with people has also meant greater mixing between wolves and domestic dogs. In some cases, wolves will prey on dogs, which ranked third in terms of their diet after carrion and sheep, according to a study carried out in northern Spain. But as wolf populations become more isolated, and individuals are cut off from each other, so there is a tendency for wolves to mate with bigger domestic dogs. Resulting hybrid offspring have been recorded in countries throughout southern Europe.

Dogs tend to range more freely here than elsewhere, and scavenge, just like the remaining wolves in some areas, so increasing liaisons are therefore likely in the future. This raises serious problems for the conservation of wolves in southern Europe. It is now doubtful whether wolves could survive here without indirect human assistance. In Italy, Spain and Portugal, studies have revealed that between 80 and 90 per cent of the diet of grey wolves is derived from a combination of farmstock and human refuse, rather than their natural prey.

Effective education of people is essential to ensure the continued existence of the wolf in Europe. Fears about wolves need to be addressed in a rational and responsible way. Recent television programmes have helped to correct the many myths which surround the wolf, but local campaigns, in areas where wolves are under threat, are most significant. The growing public awareness about environmental concerns may well be a factor which has allowed the wolf a respite in several European countries over the past 15 years or so, to the extent that numbers have grown, albeit only marginally.

Governments have a key role to play, in conjunction with conservation bodies. People must be encouraged to accept wolves, and a fair compensation scheme is an essential part of obtaining co-operation from those most directly affected by wolves within farming communities. Without such recompense for losses of stock, the hunting and poisoning of Europe's wolves will continue. Protective legislation alone is not the answer, simply because it cannot be enforced consistently.

It is possible that in localities where wolves still occur, ecotourism could be developed. Spain, for example, is a popular destination for holiday-makers from all parts of Europe, and organized trips to see wolves in the wild, along with other wildlife could be just as popular as nature holidays elsewhere in the world. Tours of this type involving wolves are a feature of some Canadian national parks.

This approach would also provide scope for the reintroduction of wild ungulates. In parts of Old Castile, a noticeable increase in the numbers of wolves has followed the reintroduction of red deer, coupled with a natural return of both roe deer (*Capreolus capreolus*) and wild boar. The other clear advantage of this approach is that it then lessens the likelihood of attacks on farmstock by wolves deprived of their natural prey.

It has also been suggested that in some areas, limited sport hunting of wolves could help to compensate farmers for loss of stock. This activity would clearly need to be tightly regulated, however. Nevertheless, in some European localities, this method of control could be used to stabilize populations, and also to remove wolf–dog hybrids.

The reintroduction of wolves is probably the most contentious problem associated with wild canids. Nevertheless, this will ultimately represent the only way of re-establishing populations in certain areas, and may be vital to link existing groups that are presently isolated.

Clearly, a reintroduction scheme is only likely to work in an area where the causes which led to the initial elimination of the wolf have been removed. The difficulties involved are illustrated by the accidental release of five male and four female wolves into an area of the Bavarian Forest in 1976. Despite an adequate supply of natural prey in the region, the wolves failed to breed and

Pack members will most commonly howl after making a successful kill.

were all dead within 2 years of their escape, with the last one being shot just across the border in Czechoslovakia.

The legislative problems facing any potential reintroduction scheme have recently been highlighted by the proposed release of grey wolves into the Yellowstone National Park. These plans have been fiercely challenged by livestock farmers in particular, fearful of attacks on their stock by wolves straying out of the park boundaries. Already facing heavy losses from coyotes, which are said to kill about 45,000 lambs annually in the state of Wyoming alone, the farmers are naturally reluctant to allow the reintroduction of wolves to their area. Despite this opposition, a wolf recovery plan was approved in 1987, and subsequently, in 1991, the US Fish and Wildlife Service was directed by Congress to prepare an Environmental Impact statement, setting out the way in which compensation claims from farmers whose stock had been attacked by wolves would be handled, as well as the degree of protection afforded to wolves which stray outside the confines of the park. The final report, on which the decision about reintroduction will be based, is set for completion in 1994.

Adult wolves eat between 2.5 and 6 kg (5½–13 lb) of food each day on average, and a typical pack comprises 2–12 individuals. The size of prey influences the size of the pack, with packs being correspondingly larger when confronting prey species such as moose. In areas where smaller prey is regularly caught, then wolves may live singly, or in pairs, as through the Arabian peninsula.

As food becomes scarce in any region, both pack size and home range show a corresponding decrease. The range can cover an area of 13,000 km^2 (5000 square miles) in parts of Alaska.

113

The social structure within a wolf pack is complex, and there is always a strict hierarchy – 'pecking order' – based ultimately on submission to the strongest male. Younger individuals constantly seek to improve their status within this hierarchy, and are ready to assert themselves as soon as an older wolf shows any sign of weakness. When the leader himself is overthrown, having been challenged or even killed by a strong younger wolf, there is often a significant reshuffling throughout the pack as the new leader takes over.

Within any one wolf pack only the leader and his mate – the dominant pair – are likely to breed. Their aggressive behaviour deters other members of the pack from mating, ensuring the best chances of survival for the leader's cubs. Mating takes place during the winter months, between January and April. The gestation period is typically around 63 days and on average six cubs are born, although up to 11 have been recorded. The female gives birth in an underground den or small cave. This is often at the end of a long tunnel, just wide enough at the entrance for the wolf to crawl in and becoming larger further along the passageway. The cubs are weaned soon after 2 months of age, with other members of the pack acting as helpers, providing food for the youngsters.

Young wolves may leave the pack when they are about a year old, adopting a solitary lifestyle for a period. In due course, they may pair up and establish a territory. The interim period is fraught with danger, however, and solitary wolves are wary not only of human contact but also of coming across other wolf packs and their territory.

There is considerable variation in the size as well as the coloration of grey wolves (*Canis lupus*) in different parts of their distribution.

Under normal circumstances, pack members keep in touch with each other by howling. They may not always respond to the calls of a neighbouring pack, because this reveals their position, leaving them open to attack. If the pack has recently made a kill, however, then it will almost inevitably reply to their neighbours, with a view to defending their food source if necessary. Scent-marking is also used to establish territorial claims, especially at the site of food caches.

Some wolf territories may be maintained for over a decade, provided that food supplies remain constant. There is usually a barrier zone between adjacent packs, if no natural division exists. Trespassing into an adjacent territory is a risky strategy, liable to result in serious fighting and mortalities, but may occur when a pack is facing starvation. Should a dominant wolf in one pack be killed at this stage, this group of wolves is likely to break up, leaving the other pack to take over their former territory. At close quarters, body language is a very important feature of communication between wolves.

On average, grey wolves are likely to live between 8 and 16 years, although they have lived for 20 years in captivity. Perhaps no other wild canid faces a more uncertain future than the wolf. In conclusion, it is worth noting that no less than seven subspecies have become extinct in less than a century. The Great Plains wolf (*Canis lupus nubilus*) is a typical example. This distinctive race used to follow the huge herds of buffalo (bison) (*Bison bison*) which thundered across the plains of North America. They were slaughtered, like their natural quarry, in massive numbers between 1850 and 1870. By the 1930s, the Great Plains wolf was extinct.

Not all surrendered meekly, however; some became wary of the poisoned carcasses left out by the hunters and became adept at avoiding traps or travelled for over 80 km (50 miles) to escape from a hunting party. The nicknames given to these individuals reflect the grudging respect that they earned from their pursuers. There was the Traveller, Three Toes of the Devil, and perhaps the most famous of all, the Custer Wolf which carried a bounty of $500 on its head. It is this resourcefulness on the part of the wolf that gives greatest encouragement to those working to assist its conservation. Here is a species that can adapt, whatever the circumstances, provided that it can be freed, at least partially, from constant human persecution.

Red wolf *Canis rufus*

DISTRIBUTION
Formerly used to range throughout the south-eastern part of the USA, from central parts of Texas south to Florida. A reintroduced population now exists in North Carolina, but this species is otherwise extinct in the wild.

In spite of its name, the red wolf can display considerable variation in coloration. It tends to be a combination of cinnamon and tawny shades, with black and grey hairs also evident in the coat. The underparts are lighter in coloration. Melanistic individuals, which are entirely black, have also been documented in the past. Overall, the red wolf is smaller than its grey cousin, weighing between 16 and 41 kg (35 and 90 lb). Other anatomical distinctions can be observed, with the red wolf having longer and more slender canines, and a more prominent sagittal crest on the skull. The rostrum or snout area is also larger.

Even so, there is doubt about the taxonomic validity of the red wolf as a distinct species. Some authorities feel that it should be regarded as a subspecies of the grey wolf (*Canis lupus*), in spite of the fact that there is no recent evidence that this species ranged into this area, while skeletal remains indicate that the red wolf was long-established in its former haunts. This also appears to rule out the suggestion that red wolves resulted from hybridization between coyotes (*Canis latrans*) and grey wolves.

Even so, there is no doubt that the red wolf and coyote hybridized quite readily in the past. This was first noted in central Texas during 1915, and appears to have become more prevalent, as numbers of red wolves declined. The suggestion that coyotes and red wolves belong to the same species is ruled out by the fact that there is no natural overlap in size between the skulls of the two, those of the latter being distinctly larger.

Nevertheless, there has clearly been mixing within the surviving red wolf population left alive today. Animals from the eastern part of the range were noticeably larger than their western counterparts, and were essentially tawny

The red wolf (*Canis rufus*) is the most endangered of all canids, with captive-breeding having been essential for its continued survival. Its future back in the wild is still uncertain.

Distribution of the red wolf (*Canis rufus*) with its last stronghold indicated by the arrow.

in colour. Those occurring in Florida and other western areas tended to be grey, with melanistic individuals being relatively common here. These divisions are no longer as clear-cut in the surviving individuals.

The decline of the red wolf has been attributed to a range of factors. Habitat destruction undoubtedly played a part, as did human persecution. Hybridization with coyotes resulted in such animals taking over areas formerly occupied by red wolves, and diluting the genes of the remaining pure wolves.

As their range declined, so the incidence of pup mortality grew, because of increasing exposure to hookworm in the relatively moist areas, such as the coastal plain of Texas, which was one of their last strongholds. Here they extended from Orange County southwards to the vicinity of Brazoria County, south of the town of Galveston.

The first serious move to save the red wolf was made in 1967, when the species was accorded endangered status by the US government. Even so, it has since become the rarest species of wild canid in the world. During 1973, a captive-breeding programme was established for the species, with groups being kept at various zoos, notably Tacoma Park Zoo, in Tacoma, Washington State. This was carried out under the auspices of the Red Wolf Committee, who also arranged for the captive population to be examined, with a view to determining how many were, in fact, pure red wolves.

Out of 40 individuals which were caught in the wild for this purpose during the 1970s, only 17 proved to be true examples of the species. By 1975, it had become increasingly clear that the species would not survive in the wild, and

117

so efforts were made to catch the remaining wolves, and develop the captive-breeding programme. In 1980, the red wolf was then deemed to be extinct in the wild.

The tiny residual population in captivity began to breed in 1977. Subsequently, numbers have increased well, with a current population of over 130 red wolves, held at more than 20 localities through the USA. A release scheme began in 1988, when eight of these wolves were released into the Alligator River National Wildlife Refuge in North Carolina. Two pairs then bred in the following year, and although some have been killed, the project appears to be proceeding reasonably well, giving hope for the survival of the species both here and elsewhere in the country.

In the longer term, however, the shortage of genetic diversity within the founder stock could pose problems, leading to poor reproductive potential, while the spread of the coyote is clearly another hazard. Estimates suggest that about 90 per cent of the former territory of the red wolf is now populated by coyotes, with the risk of continued hybridization posing a serious threat.

Red wolves live in small family packs, and the social structure of the groups in release areas is an important consideration. Although they will take deer, their natural quarry is generally smaller, being comprised of raccoons (*Procyon lotor*), swamp rabbits (*Sylvilagus aquaticus*) and the introduced coypu (nutria) (*Myocastor coypus*).

Breeding details are very similar to those of the grey wolf, with mating again taking place early in the year. Their dens may be concealed above ground in hollow trees, or excavated in the banks of streams or similar localities, extending back a distance of about 2.4 m (7½ ft). They are relatively shallow structures, sited no more than 1 m (3 ft) below ground.

Raccoon dog *Nyctereutes procyonoides*

DISTRIBUTION
Native to south-eastern Siberia, Manchuria, northern Indo-China, China and Japan. Introduced initially to the western part of the former USSR, it has since spread westwards into Scandinavia and via Germany into France.

In terms of its appearance, the raccoon dog is a most uncharacteristic canid. As its name suggests, it looks more like a raccoon, with its short legs, thick-set body and distinctive facial markings. The coloration of the raccoon dog's fur is variable, being typically blackish-brown. Its profusely furred tail tends to be dark and short, accounting for less than one-third of body length. The fur on the legs is also usually darker than that on the body.

Raccoon dogs have no close relatives within the family Canidae, although they would appear to show both behavioural and anatomical links with the bat-eared fox (*Otocyon megalotis*). In contrast to most canids, raccoon dogs are found in heavily wooded areas, often close to water. They have a varied diet, being truly omnivorous in their feeding habits. Their food intake depends on the area and season, but small animals, ranging from rodents and lizards to frogs and ground-dwelling birds are frequent prey. They will also eat seeds, fruit and berries, particularly during the autumn, as well as invertebrates.

Raccoon dogs (*Nyctereutes procyonoides*) appear to be more similar to raccoons than canids at first glance, with their characteristic facial markings and small ears.

The lack of large prey in the diet is reflected in the pattern of dentition. The teeth of raccoon dogs are relatively small, and the arrangement of the carnassial teeth, used for chewing bones, is significantly reduced. The molars, on the other hand, are enlarged for grinding up plant material.

Raccoon dogs are also able to eat amphibians such as toads, which are normally protected by their toxic skin secretions. They achieve this by producing copious quantities of saliva, which dilutes the toxins.

A distinct seasonal pattern exists in the case of the raccoon dog. As autumn approaches, they start to put on weight, up from 4–6 kg (9–13 lb), to 6–10 kg (13–22 lb). They will then retreat to their burrow, and rest through the winter, relying on their stores of fat to nourish them over this period. This commences in November in Japan, and may last until the following April, although they do not undergo a period of complete hibernation. If the weather is mild, for example, the raccoon dogs may emerge and start feeding, while in the milder southern parts of their range, they may not sleep for any significant period of time.

Soon after they emerge, mating takes place. Raccoon dogs tend to live in pairs, with the female being in oestrus for about 6 days. When mating takes place, the tie is quite short, lasting for approximately 6 minutes. Assuming fertilization occurs, about five pups are likely to be born, although much larger litters comprising up to 12 young have been recorded. Male raccoon dogs help to provide food, first for their mates, and then for their growing offspring, as they begin to take solid food. In some areas, several pairs may

119

occupy dens in close proximity to each other, establishing no strong territorial boundaries.

Raccoon dogs are largely nocturnal in their habits, starting to hunt for food soon after sunset and continuing through the night, aside from a short break usually around midnight. Only on rare occasions are they seen during the daytime. When in search of food, they may range over a distance of up to 20 km (12 miles) at night, although typically, they cover about half this distance. Where they occur close to the sea, raccoon dogs may abandon their natural caution, and wander along the shoreline, seeking crabs and any carrion washed up by the tide.

A number of predators may take raccoon dogs, including birds such as owls and golden eagles (*Aquila chrysaetos*). Lynxes (*Lynx lynx*), wolverines (*Gulo gulo*), wolves and even domestic dogs can all be dangerous. In Japan, where the species is now scarce, raccoon dogs have been heavily hunted for their meat and fur, as well as their bones which are reputed to have medicinal qualities.

Within their range, raccoon dogs establish dunging sites, which are used regularly. These can be quite conspicuous and appear to serve a territorial function, simply indicating their presence. This may be linked to the fact that unlike other canids, raccoon dogs do not bark, although they have a series of other vocalizations, some of which tend to be uttered only in specific situations, such as during mating. Another communicative peculiarity is that a dominant individual will arch its tail in an inverted 'U' shape, as confirmation of its status.

Distribution of the raccoon dog (*Nyctereutes procyonoides*).

These canids breed readily in suitable surroundings, with males helping the females with the rearing of their offspring. This pair is part of a breeding group in Poznan Zoo, Poland.

Young raccoon dogs are mature by a year old. In the wild, their lifespan is little more than 3 years on average, but it can be as long as 11 years in captivity. They are widely kept for their fur, and this has led to the establishment of an expanding wild population in Europe.

The first introduction of raccoon dogs into Europe took place about 1928, when 415 females, all of which were thought to be pregnant, were released at various localities in the former USSR. In view of the involvement of the male in the rearing of young, it is perhaps not surprising that this release scheme was not an overwhelming success. Today, their descendants are confined to a small area of forest between the Sulak and Terek Rivers in the Dagestan ASSR. These are of the Siberian race (*N. procyonoides ussuriensis*).

Other releases followed, however, with 8651 raccoon dogs being introduced to various localities in European Russia between 1929 and 1967. Here they prey mainly upon hares, game birds and poultry, adapting their diet because of competition from native mustelids. From Russia they soon spread into Finland, reaching here about 1935, and since World War 2, they have moved further westwards as well as southwards. Their spread through Poland was achieved at a maximum rate of 300 km (186 miles) per annum, after they were first sighted here in 1955. They had reached Germany by the 1960s, crossing the French border for the first time in 1979. By 1984, it was estimated that raccoon dogs had spread over an area of 1.4 million km^2 (540,000 square miles) from their original sites of release in Europe.

Although they have a less developed brain than other canids, this does not appear to have handicapped their movements here. It is likely that they will continue to spread across Europe, using whatever shelter is available to conceal their presence during the daytime.

121

In mainland Asia, raccoon dogs have spread naturally into Mongolia, from western parts of China. Here they first appeared around Mount Choibalsan and Lake Buir at the start of the 1960s, although there appear to be no recent reports of their status here. Hunting of raccoon dogs is widespread in Japan, with an estimated 70,000 being killed annually, and the species is apparently declining at an increasing rate.

Grey fox (tree-climbing fox) *Urocyon cinereoargenteus*

DISTRIBUTION
Occurs over much of the USA, extending to the border with Canada, although not found further south in the Rockies or in the north-western states. Small populations now exist again in southern Canada. Further south, it ranges through Central America down to northern parts of South America, occurring in both Colombia and Venezuela.

The coloration of the grey fox is more variable than its name would suggest, being silvery-grey offset against shades of reddish-yellow, most noticeably on the legs. Individuals from the northern part of the range tend to be more colourful than those found further south. Since they live in a relatively warm part of the world, these foxes do not have a dense undercoat, and their fur is relatively coarse.

Their legs are short compared with those of the red fox (*Vulpes vulpes*), and they stand about 36 cm (14 in) tall at the shoulder. An unusual feature of the grey fox is that its pupils are oval in shape, rather than slit-like, as in *Vulpes* species.

Grey foxes are adaptable creatures and can be found in a wide variety of environments, often ranging close to towns and cities. Their dens are well-concealed, and may be located in trees, up to 9 m (30 ft) off the ground. Unlike other canids, grey foxes are agile climbers, although in northern parts of their range, they prefer to live in underground burrows. They rarely dig these themselves, however, usually choosing to occupy abandoned dens of other species.

Here they hide away during the daytime, emerging at night to hunt small mammals and birds, which form the bulk of their diet. Grey foxes rarely attack domestic poultry, and insects form a significant part of their food intake. They will also eat a variety of fruit and vegetable matter. Their feeding habits differ in various parts of their range; in the Zion National Park, Utah, for example, they are essentially insectivorous and herbivorous, rather than carnivorous.

The oestrus period is influenced by the latitude, being earlier in the southern USA than further north, where females may not mate until the middle of May in New York State. A pair will then stay together, with the female giving birth after a gestation period of about 59 days to an average of four cubs, although as many as 10 have been recorded on occasions. The pups are black in colour at birth, and it is 6 weeks before they are weaned. The young foxes will be hunting on their own by the time they reach 4 months of

The grey fox (*Urocyon cinereoargenteus*) often retreats into trees to avoid danger, and so is sometimes known as the tree-climbing fox.

Distribution of the grey fox (*Urocyon cinereoargenteus*).

age, although they will stay within their parents' territory until the start of the following year.

If threatened, grey foxes will rarely run off, but tend instead to seek shelter, often by climbing trees, using the long claws on their hind feet to anchor themselves on to the trunk, while reaching higher with their forepaws. Once danger has passed, they reverse down the tree backwards.

The absence of the grey fox from the Great Plains is a reflection of the fact that this area has almost no tree cover. The same applies in the desert region of the USA, where it is replaced by the swift fox (*Vulpes velox*). Extensive deforestation for agricultural purposes in north-eastern USA has also led to a decline in its numbers here.

In Canada, where the grey fox became extinct towards the end of the seventeenth century, it appears to be recolonizing parts of its former range. The species has been observed in areas of Quebec, Manitoba and southern Ontario. This may be linked to the spread of rabbits here. It has been suggested that the introduction of the red fox (*Vulpes vulpes*) was responsible for the decline of this species in Canada, but it now appears this is less likely to have been the reason. Studies suggest that grey foxes are dominant to both red and Arctic (*Alopex lagopus*) foxes in areas where they occur together.

Grey foxes may fall victim to other larger canids such as coyotes, however, and pumas (*Felis concolor*) will also prey upon them. Large raptors such as eagles take a toll on their numbers, especially pups, and large numbers are also killed for their fur. The demand for grey fox fur has grown dramatically

124

over the past decade, with nearly half a million currently being trapped annually to meet this market.

In the state of Wisconsin, it is estimated that half the state's grey fox population is killed annually for the fur trade. Even so, the relatively prolific nature of this species suggests that this level of offtake is not endangering it at present, although the situation needs careful monitoring.

Island grey fox *Urocyon littoralis*

DISTRIBUTION
Formerly thought to occur only on the six largest of the eight Channel Islands, located off the coast of southern California: San Miguel, San Nicolas, Santa Cruz, San Clemente, Santa Catalina and Santa Rosa. It has recently been suggested that some neighbouring mainland populations are of this species.

The status of these grey foxes has long been a subject for debate, but zoologists are now agreed that it should be recognized as a species in its own right, in spite of its close similarity to the grey fox (*U. cinereoargenteus*). They have a restricted habitat, with Santa Cruz, the largest of these islands, being just 38 km (23 miles) in length and between 3 and 13 km (2–8 miles) in width.

Island grey foxes are smaller than the grey fox itself, and can also be distinguished easily by their shorter tails, which have two less vertebrae.

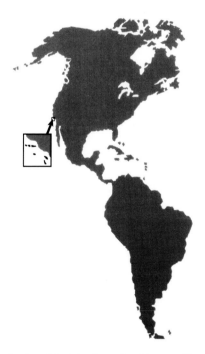

Distribution of the island grey fox (*Urocyon littoralis*).

Their ancestors crossed to the islands when the northern group comprised a single land mass, during the late Pleistocene, less than one million years ago. It is possible that they were rafted here on trees washed out to sea, bearing in mind that they can anchor firmly on to trunks. They would have travelled about 6.5 km (4 miles). The introduction of these foxes to the southern islands, on the other hand, appears to have been carried out by people, about 10,000 years ago. Young foxes can become quite tame, and may well have been kept as pets. A pair of these foxes may also have been taken in 1875 from Santa Catalina to San Clemente, although they were already present here by this time.

Island grey foxes feed largely on insects, as well as fruit when available. They will also catch small mammals, although these are not numerous, and take reptiles, as well as birds and their eggs on occasions.

The population densities vary widely, although overall, they are found at higher densities than the grey fox. There are less than 0.3 foxes per km^2 (0.3 square miles) on Santa Catalina, where the species is scarce, up to nearly eight in the same area on Santa Cruz. Scats are often used to indicate territorial boundaries, along with scent-marking.

These foxes are active during the day, especially from the later part of the afternoon through to the early evening, although they tend to be seen more often at other times during the winter period.

Their breeding period is fairly consistent, with pairs coming together in January. Mating then occurs around the middle of March, with the pups being born in late April or early May. Litter size is relatively small, averaging just over two pups per pair, with a maximum of five being recorded. This may be related to the fact that these foxes tend to have a longer lifespan on these islands, being relatively free from predators, as well as disease.

In fact, a survey of 100 island grey foxes has revealed that they had not been exposed to leptospirosis, distemper or rabies, and more significantly, in terms of their conservation, they have no protection against these infections. Potentially, the effect of a sick dog reaching one of the islands where these foxes are found could be devastating. As a priority, the introduction of other animals to these islands must therefore be prevented.

Island grey foxes are already strictly protected, and benefit from their remote location in this respect. The National Park Service controls the islands of San Miguel and Santa Rosa, while San Nicolas and San Clemente are administered by the US Navy. Here steps are being taken to eliminate the feral cats found on these two islands, which could compete with the foxes for food.

The human impact on the environment has also provided additional food, however, with up to 20 foxes being observed scavenging on rubbish dumps for food. They do not appear to quarrel greatly, even between September and December, when pairs have broken up and their youngsters have dispersed.

Research is now underway to investigate the genetics of the island grey fox. This work should also help to shed some light on its relationship with its mainland relative, and determine whether in fact a separate population of island grey foxes does indeed occur here. This could have important conservation implications, given the resulting difference in disease status between them.

Swift fox (kit fox; prairie fox) *Vulpes velox*

Now confined to the western part of the United States; formerly occurred in Canada ranging from southern Alberta and Saskatchewan, as well as possibly south-west Manitoba southwards across the border as far as north-west Texas. Now being reintroduced to parts of Canada.

The taxonomy of this species is controversial: some zoologists consider that the 'true' kit fox should be accorded specific status, under the name of *Vulpes macrotis*, rather than being listed as a subspecies of *V. velox*. There is a difference between the northern plains form, with its smaller ears and dark coat, and the desert-dwelling variety occurring in the south and west.

What is beyond doubt is the fact that these foxes have declined in numbers, particularly in northern parts of their range. The San Joaquin kit fox (*V. velox mutica*) is considered to be endangered, being reduced to a population of around 7000 individuals in California. Hunting probably contributed to the disappearance of the species in Canada, as it used to be widely trapped for its fur.

More recently, it has been suggested that the use of '1080' poisons to curb the numbers of coyotes (*Canis latrans*) may have contributed to the decline of this species in California. The state has now banned such chemicals unless it can be proven that the San Joaquin kit fox does not occur in the area. They have not been used on land under federal control since 1972, and here it

Distribution of the swift fox (*Vulpes velox*).

appears that kit foxes are undergoing a revival in numbers. Such poisons are used to curb the numbers of coyotes (*Canis latrans*), but unfortunately, kit foxes are far less wary, and are more likely to take poisoned bait.

Coyotes will also kill these small foxes, and so in areas where coyote numbers are controlled the fox population has a better chance of survival. Kit foxes may be adversely affected by the poisoning of rodents as well, either directly or because this creates a shortage of prey for them. They are primarily carnivorous in their feeding habits, taking both lagomorphs and rodents as the main item in their diet. Insects are also eaten, especially crickets, as well as cactus fruits in some areas. Birds do not appear to feature prominently as prey species, but may be taken on occasions.

When food is plentiful, kit foxes will cache any surplus. Hunting takes place essentially at night, when the desert temperature is lower, with the foxes resting in their dens during the daytime. These are usually excavated in areas where there may be little cover available, about 1 m (3 ft) below the surface. The network of tunnels may extend back 4 m (13 ft) or more.

Kit foxes do not display strong territorial instincts, and overlapping home ranges are common. The only evidence of marking is with scats close to the burrow; scent-marking is not used to indicate territorial boundaries in this species.

Pairs are established by late winter, with the resulting offspring being born typically between February and April. The number of pups in a litter appears to correlate with the available prey in an area, and if the population density approaches the maximum carrying capacity of the habitat, then proportionately more male offspring are likely to be born.

Males play an important part in the successful rearing of a litter, by obtaining food for their mates before the pups are weaned. Both parents will then start hunting to feed their offspring, but it will not be until the pups are at least 3 months old that they will start to accompany the adult foxes on hunting excursions.

The family breaks up around October, and pups may travel 32 km (19 miles) at this stage, based on tagging studies. They will not necessarily breed during the following year. The small size of these foxes leaves them vulnerable to birds of prey, such as red-tailed hawks (*Buteo jamaicensis*), and it seems unlikely that they will live for more than about 7 years in the wild, based upon the limited data available, although individuals have lived for 20 years in captivity.

Attempts to reintroduce these foxes to Canada started in the early 1980s, with the release of 246 taking place between 1984 and 1988. Seventeen sites were chosen, with the majority being located in Alberta, and five in Saskatchewan. At first, the foxes were held in pens for a period before release, but starting in 1987, the so-called 'hard release' system was used, simply turning them loose, with this project being controlled by the Canadian Wildlife Service. Initial results were particularly encouraging, with seven litters producing 33 pups that were weaned successfully during 1988. The scheme is not without controversy, however, because of the use of foxes from the south for this purpose.

Nevertheless, there is some evidence that southern foxes may be pushing north naturally in some areas. For example, the kit fox was thought to have become extinct in Montana, where the northern subspecies *V. velox hebes* occurred. Then after an absence of 70 years, a sighting took place here during 1978. Similarly, the species is breeding again in South Dakota, about 60 years after it was last reported. These intervals suggest recolonization from further south, rather than the species remaining undetected here throughout this period. Currently, it appears that numbers in northern areas are now increasing again, or are at least stable in many cases.

Red fox *Vulpes vulpes*

DISTRIBUTION
Ranges over most of the northern hemisphere above the line of latitude marking 30°N, except for the Arctic. In North America, the range of the red fox extends as far south as central Texas at present. It occurs throughout Europe and most of Asia, apart from the south-east. Populations also occur in North Africa, and in Australia and some Pacific islands, where these foxes were introduced during the nineteenth century.

While the social living arrangements and hunting techniques of the grey wolf (*Canis lupus*) have meant that it has become extinct in much of its former range, owing to human development and persecution, the red fox has adapted to fill this niche. It has now become the most widely distributed canid, with a massive natural range, capable of living alongside people in some of the most densely populated cities on earth, including Paris and London.

As described earlier (page 23), red foxes were introduced to Australia in the nineteenth century in an attempt to control the rabbit population. They were also introduced from Europe to the east coast of the USA as early as the seventeenth century, but here it was for foxhunting purposes. From the east coast they spread south-east and west, across the Great Plains, and are now common in agricultural areas. Some mixing with the native North American stock, which originally only inhabited the north-east of the country, has occurred.

Red foxes are found in a very wide range of habitats, although they usually avoid desert regions or heavily wooded coniferous areas. Nevertheless, there is a population established in the arid, sandy region of north-west India.

The red fox is the largest member of the genus *Vulpes*, although there is a considerable range in size through its distribution. Males are invariably heavier than females, and those living in northern areas tend to be the biggest, weighing up to 14 kg (30 lb), although individuals of more than 10 kg (22 lb) are decidedly uncommon. While many red foxes do in fact have a predominantly rufous coat, there can also be a significant individual variation in coloration (see page 39).

As might be expected from a species that ranges over such a wide area, red foxes are highly opportunistic in their feeding habits. Although rodents and other small animals naturally form the bulk of their diet, they will also scavenge, particularly in urban areas where, relatively free from persecution, they have become bolder, and may be seen regularly in gardens or parks during the daytime.

Distribution of the red fox (*Vulpes vulpes*).

Red foxes rarely prey on animals weighing more than 3 kg (6½ lb), but will take young lambs, roe deer (*Capreolus capreolus*) and even wild boar (*Sus scrofa*) up to this size. Their daily food intake varies between 0.5 to 1 kg (1–2 lb), and any surplus will be cached or stored within their den. In the autumn, vegetables, fruit and berries are eaten in large quantities, including cultivated crops such as turnips and cabbage.

The size of the home range is variable, and tends to be smaller in urban areas, where foxes are less vulnerable to persecution. It tends to average between 2 and 5 km^2 (0.7–1.9 square miles), but can fall anywhere within a range from 0.1 to 20 km^2 (0.04–8 square miles), depending on the availability of food.

Both sexes mark their territory, using both urine and faeces. The usual social arrangement takes the form of a mated pair, sometimes accompanied by their offspring, although a number of variations on this pattern have been recorded. The most usual of these is a single dog fox accompanied by several vixens, of which one is dominant. They are usually related. Only the dominant female breeds, with the other vixen assisting with the care of the cubs. The group tends to be highly territorial, excluding foxes from neighbouring areas. They will usually defend their home range from incursions, attacking any intruder fiercely.

The mating season extends between December and April, and is influenced to some degree by the latitude, occurring earlier in the south. In some parts of the world, the conception rate depends on the availability of prey. In central and northern parts of Sweden, for example, the percentage of vixens giving birth is influenced by the availability of voles (*Clethrionomys rutilus*), which are

130

Red foxes (*Vulpes vulpes*) are often to be found in gardens, where they live close to people. This den site is under a garden shed.

The red fox (*Vulpes vulpes*) is now the most widely distributed of all wild canids, possessing a highly opportunistic nature.

In spite of its reputation for killing poultry, the red fox (*Vulpes vulpes*) often seeks out fruit such as blackberries to eat in the autumn.

their main prey. These rodents have a distinctive population cycle, and the highest number of fox cubs will be produced as the numbers of voles grow rapidly, before crashing. Here in the spruce forests of the far north, there is little other food for the foxes.

A similar phenomenon has been observed in North America, where the number of breeding vixens has been found to be related to the price paid for fox pelts. As the price rises, the intensity of hunting increases and more foxes are killed. However, because up to 30 per cent of the population are non-breeding females, a relatively large number can be killed without harming the reproductive potential of the community. In fact, with more food available for the survivors, an increase in breeding is possible and the population is soon boosted to its previous level.

The vixen will give birth to her offspring in a den. This may be dug by the foxes themselves, in a concealed locality, or they may use a burrow abandoned by another animal, adapting it to their needs. The den may evolve into a fairly complex structure, being used by numerous generations of foxes over many years. One such den is known to have been inhabited for over 35 years, but in some cases, a vixen may move her cubs to another den before they are independent.

Typically, 3 or 4 cubs will be born, but as many as 12 have been recorded. If more than one vixen gives birth in the den, then they will share the task of bringing up their offspring, with the male assisting by providing food. The group will remain together until the autumn, with the cubs being fully weaned by 2 months old.

Male red foxes tend to leave the family first, from 6 months of age onwards. They also travel greater distances, up to 30 km (18 miles), than the female siblings, some of whom may stay in the area of their birth, and establish their own territories. Red foxes are mature by about 10 months old, and will breed the following year. Males unable to establish a territory are likely to die before long, being vulnerable to starvation and predation. As winter approaches, so the calls of male foxes exerting territorial claims can be heard with increasing frequency after dark.

Red foxes rarely survive much beyond 3 years, although potentially they could live for up to 12 years. They suffer a high level of mortality for a variety of reasons. Human persecution, either shooting, hunting or trapping takes a toll on their numbers, while in urban areas in particular, many foxes die on the roads, as the result of collisions with vehicles.

Diseases, notably rabies, kill many red foxes, while parasitic ailments such as mange, which are easily transmitted by direct contact in dens can also prove fatal, particularly in the case of animals suffering from hunger and cold.

Other canids, such as dingoes (*Canis familiaris dingo*) in Australia, and both wolves and coyotes (*Canis latrans*) in North America also prey upon red foxes. In the state of Alberta, these foxes only occur in areas where coyotes are absent, and a similar situation also exists in both North Dakota and Maine, although elsewhere there appears to be less conflict.

Red foxes, especially cubs, may also be preyed upon occasionally by golden eagles (*Aquila chrysaetos*) and other large birds of prey in relatively open areas of country. Even so, they will put up a determined challenge when pursued, breaking from their usual trot into a gallop, which they can maintain over a considerable distance.

Their agility means that they are also hard to corner, as they can jump some distance off the ground, on to a tree branch or leap over a wall to escape if necessary. Red foxes will also take to water readily to throw hounds off the scent, although they are not natural swimmers.

Their hearing is especially acute, enabling them to detect potential danger at an early stage. When they do rest briefly in suitable cover above ground, their ears are frequently twitching to detect sounds, and it is exceedingly difficult to creep up on a fox undetected. Their keen sense of hearing also enables them to detect rodents such as mice from over 45 m (150 ft) away, helping them to hunt efficiently.

In spite of the huge numbers of red foxes that perish each year, the species continues to thrive, even in areas where human persecution is most intense. Its innate cunning, which is merely further evidence of its adaptability, means that a single fox can manage to outwit a pack of 30 or more chasing hounds. In spite of other pressures on its population in Britain, including shooting, it is estimated that there are now more red foxes here than there were during medieval times.

Chapter 7
Canids of Africa and the Middle East

This division is not an entirely separate division from the Holarctic distribution, because the red fox (*Vulpes vulpes*) does extend into this region. Similarly, the golden jackal (*Canis aureus*), although mainly found here, also occurs in the far south-east of Europe and extends across southern parts of Asia. Canids are widely distributed across Africa and the Middle East, exploiting the range of different habitats found in this part of the world, although they tend to be most numerous in areas of grassland and desert. The African wild dog (*Lycaon pictus*) does range into forested areas, however, and occurs at various altitudes.

Side-striped jackal *Canis adustus*

DISTRIBUTION
Tropical parts of Africa; known to occur in Nigeria in the west, as well as the Gambia, and eastwards to southern Sudan, Ethiopia, and southwards via Kenya and Tanzania. Present across much of the lower third of the continent, apart from the south, reaching northern Namibia and Kwazulu and Natal provinces in the Transvaal.

The precise range of this species is not fully documented, particularly in West Africa, because of the difficulties in observing these canids. They are found in well-wooded terrain, and sometimes in swampy areas, and are the most widespread of all jackals.

The side-striped jackal is so-called because of the paler line of guard hairs running along the sides of its body, extending from the vicinity of the shoulder to the base of the tail. Overall, they have a more lupine appearance than other jackals, with a broader and shorter muzzle.

The omnivorous nature of their diet is reflected by their dentition, with their molars being larger than those of other jackals, while the carnassial teeth are reduced in size. Studies carried out in northern Botswana indicate that in agricultural areas here, these jackals consume vegetables as a major part of their diet, along with invertebrates and rodents. They may also feed on carrion but do not pose a threat to livestock.

Side-striped jackals are relatively quiet by nature, uttering just a series of single barks, and do not howl like their relatives. They are not commonly seen, being essentially nocturnal, although they can sometimes be observed during the daytime when the weather is relatively cool.

They may live singly, although they tend to associate as pairs, and then as family groups after the breeding period. Larger groups, comprised of up to a

Distribution of the side-striped jackal (*Canis adustus*).

dozen individuals may be observed occasionally, feeding on carrion after a lion kill for example. They may be encountered up to altitudes of 2700 m (8858 ft).

Breeding occurs at different times of the year throughout their range, with births occurring during the winter period in southern Africa. The female gives birth in an underground den, favouring a disused tunnel dug by aardvarks (*Orycteropus afer*), or an old termites' nest for this purpose. The gestation is relatively long, typically lasting between 57 and 70 days, with an average litter being comprised of three or four pups, although as many as seven have been recorded on occasions.

Suckling lasts up to 10 weeks, and the young will be sexually mature by the time they disperse, at nearly a year old. Males can be recognized by their larger size, weighing an average of 9.4 kg (21 lb), making them about 1 kg (2 lb) heavier than females.

In some areas, all three species of African jackal can occur together. The division between them began about 2 million years ago. The side-striped is the biggest, and although the stripes running along the sides of the body are usually distinctive, they may be relatively inconspicuous in some individuals. Similarly, although the tip of the tail is generally white this is not a universal feature; in northern populations it tends to be black. Their scientific name '*adustus*' means 'sunburned', and refers to their body coloration, which is a greyish-fawn, being lighter on the flanks and underparts.

Disease in some areas may be a threat to side-striped and other jackals, especially rabies and distemper which can flare up from time to time. They are not generally persecuted however, although in some areas, they may be hunted, with parts of their body being traditionally valued for medicinal purposes. The Buganda tribe, for example, rely on the heart of the side-striped

135

jackal for the treatment of epilepsy, while the jackal's skin and nails are reputed to keep away evil spirits.

The precise status of this species is unclear; although it is generally considered to be rare, this may be more a reflection of its secretive nature than an accurate assessment. Certainly, populations are well-represented within many protected areas, including national parks, through its range.

Golden jackal (Asiatic jackal) *Canis aureus*

DISTRIBUTION
Occurs right across north Africa, extending southwards in the east to Ethiopia, and throughout the Middle East, across Asia as far as Thailand and Burma. Also present in south-east Europe.

The golden jackal is the most widely distributed member of this group of wild canids, and may be extending its range further in some areas, notably Ethiopia, where it has recently been recorded in the south of the country, in the Harenna Forest, and also within the Bale Mountains National Park. New European reports of golden jackals have also originated from eastern Italy and north-eastern Austria during recent years, with this species occurring further north than other jackals.

The appearance of the golden jackal varies somewhat through its wide range, with its greyish-yellow fur often having a rufous tinge, particularly on the limbs. The coloration of these jackals is influenced by their habitat. They are palest in sandy, semi-desert areas, and darker elsewhere. They measure between 38 and 50 cm (15 and 20 in) at the shoulder, and weigh from 7 to 15 kg (15–33 lb), with males being significantly larger than females.

Golden jackals often frequent rather arid areas, although they are not generally found in deserts. Even so, they do occur in the Israeli desert, close to oases, and elsewhere they may range up to 4000 m (13,123 ft) above sea level, confirming the adaptability of this species. In East Africa, they favour the plains rather than wooded country, while in Europe they are found in lowland areas.

They often occur close to human settlements, although here they tend to be especially secretive by nature and are largely nocturnal. Perhaps it was their howling around the cities of Ancient Egypt that led to the incorporation of their image into the form of the god Anubis. Some representations show Anubis simply as a jackal, whereas other portrayals combine a jackal's head with a human body. There are also many references to jackals in ancient literature from this part of the world as creatures of the night, frequently linked with death, as in the case of Anubis.

Golden jackals are scavengers in part, but they are no less capable of hunting. Lagomorphs, rodents, ground-dwelling birds as well as insects and fish may all feature in their diet. They will sometimes catch domestic chicken, and have been recorded as preying upon lambs and kids in Kashmir. Young animals typically are hunted whenever possible.

In the Serengeti for example, golden jackals will prey heavily on young Thompson's gazelles (*Gazella thomsoni*) during the fawning season, which

The golden jackal (*Canis aureus*) is extending its range in some areas, including parts of Europe.

extends from January to April. At this stage young gazelles can comprise half of their diet. Newborn gazelles are relatively easy quarry. As the jackal approaches the fawn attempts to hide, concealing itself against the ground, and its mother moves off, in an attempt to distract the predator. When the jackal gets within about 9 m (30 ft), the fawn staggers to its feet and attempts to run off, while its mother returns to defend it by butting the jackal. When jackals are hunting in pairs, this defence is rarely adequate; in attempting to thwart one jackal, the gazelle leaves the way open for the second to overpower the fawn.

The remainder of the jackal's diet at this stage is largely comprised of insects, particularly dung beetles. Later in the year, however, gazelles will comprise barely a quarter of their food intake, with carrion, small mammals, birds and fruit figuring more prominently.

The pair bond is relatively strong in golden jackals. Mating tends to occur early in the year, with pregnancy lasting around 63 days. The number of offspring may be related in part to the territory. Litters on the Serengeti average only two pups, but four may be more usual elsewhere. Although generally females only produce a single litter in the course of a year, there is at least one record of a pair breeding twice in one season. This may be related to the availability of food. Up to nine pups have been produced in a single litter.

The area occupied by a pair depends to a large extent on the ease with which food can be acquired. It typically varies from 2.5 to 20 km^2 (1–8 square miles). The male golden jackal takes much of the responsibility for

Distribution of the golden jackal (*Canis aureus*).

providing for his mate and litter while they are in the den. This is not an elaborate structure, often being little more than a straight tunnel dug out at the base of a tree. Golden jackals often prefer to take over burrows dug by other species, such as porcupines (*Hystrix cristata*) or warthogs (*Phacochoerus aethiopicus*), which have been abandoned, and then adapt these for their own use.

Living alongside the breeding pair may be youngsters from the previous year. These may have wandered off for a period and then returned, to be accepted back by other members of the family group. Jackals hunting together are much more adept than those seeking prey alone, especially when pursuing larger quarry such as gazelles.

The young golden jackals will first emerge from the den when they are about 2 weeks old. The adults will start to regurgitate food for them from this point onwards, and the pups learn to beg for this by nuzzling close to the side of the adult's mouth and wagging their tails.

Assuming that food is plentiful, they develop rapidly, starting to accompany their parents on hunting expeditions by the time they are 3 months old. At first, the youngsters are more likely to prove a disturbance, but gradually they learn to master the techniques required. They may stay with the family group until the following year, with males often not breeding for the first time until they are over 2 years old.

Golden jackals are quite common through much of their range. In some areas, they have suffered from human persecution, but their presence can be beneficial, as was confirmed in Israel. Here these jackals were poisoned, and the number of human victims of snake bites in the region soared from 229 up to 435 in 2 years. This was because golden jackals regularly kill snakes, and once the poisoning campaign ceased, the number of recorded snake bites dropped back as well, as jackal numbers rose again.

Few surveys of the numbers of this species have been carried out, although in the Serengeti, it appears that their population is relatively stable, numbering about 1600 in total. Golden jackals have been recorded as living for 13 years in the wild, and up to the age of 16 in zoological collections.

Black-backed jackal (silver-backed jackal) *Canis mesomelas*

DISTRIBUTION
Two distinct populations exist in Africa. The northerly population extends from the Gulf of Aden south to Tanzania. Unconnected to this, the southern population occurs from south-west Angola, Zimbabwe and Mozambique southwards to the tip of the continent.

There is a considerable variation in the size of these jackals through their range, with the smallest individuals reportedly being found in Somalia. They can measure from 38 to 48 cm (15–19 in) at the shoulder, and from 6 to 13.5 kg (13–30 lb) in weight. Males are consistently bigger than females, being about 1 kg (2 lb) heavier.

The distinctive characteristic of the black-backed jackal is the black and silver marking running down the back, from the shoulders to the tip of the tail.

Distribution of the black-backed jackal (*Canis mesomelas*).

The tail itself is brownish, with a black tip, while the sides of the body are reddish-cream, often becoming paler on the underparts.

More common than the side-striped jackal (*C. adustus*), to which they are closely related, black-backed jackals are found in fairly open areas of countryside, particularly grassland and brushy stretches of woodland. In areas of overlap with other species of jackal, this species is most likely to be seen in open areas of woodland.

They are highly opportunistic in their feeding habits. In the southern part of their range, in some coastal areas, they will even invade Cape fur seal (*Arctocephalus pusillus*) colonies, seizing young pups and scavenging along the coastline. Further north, these canids will follow hunting lions (*Panthera leo*), eating from their kills. In fact, the black-backed tends to feed more on carrion here than its golden relative, and is bolder. Black-backed jackals may dart in among feeding hyaenas (*Hyaena hyaena*), rather than waiting for them to finish their meal.

When necessary, however, these jackals will resort to hunting, often working in pairs to achieve a kill. Gazelles are a popular target, but they may also take larger quarry, such as newly born wildebeest (*Connochaetes gnou*) calves, with one of the jackals distracting the mother, while the other seizes the youngster.

The case of co-operative hunting between black-backed jackals and a cheetah has already been described (see page 60). This was observed in the Nairobi Park; the jackals acted as a distraction, which enabled the cheetah to move in very close, greatly increasing the likelihood of a successful kill.

The sheep-killing activities of these jackals, in particular during the lambing season, has led to their persecution in southern Africa. In some areas here, pastures are enclosed to deter jackal attacks, particularly when valuable caracul sheep – which provide the so-called Persian lamb pelts – are involved. Even so, the extent of predation by jackals here is probably exaggerated, with many of the sheep being killed by domestic dogs rather than jackals.

Black-backed jackals are found in pairs throughout the year, and they may also associate in family groups as well. A study of the population in the Natal Drakensberg, South Africa, revealed that a quarter of the jackals here were paired, and a further quarter were young, less than a year old. The bulk were non-breeding adults, a number of which were living as helpers. This assistance can help to increase the number of offspring reared successfully quite significantly.

Pairing occurs several months before mating, and although youngsters will be mature by a year old, they may not breed for a further year. In the southern part of their range, mating can occur from April to July, whereas in Tanzania, this period extends from about the middle of July through until September. Males may fight viciously in order to obtain a mate, but the female selects her partner.

The den is again likely to be the result of excavatory work by another creature such as an aardvark (*Orycteropus afer*), which has been adapted by the jackals. Termite mounds are favoured in some areas, notably the Serengeti. The litter size will probably be influenced by the age of the female, with young and old individuals usually having no more than three pups in a litter. Up to eight may be born in other cases, but mortality in the critical early weeks of life is often high, leaving barely half alive.

Food shortages are a threat, and trotting at about 8 km per hour (5 mph) males may cover distances of 40 km (25 miles) or more in a night, searching for food for their family. This is where helpers can be of great value, increasing the likelihood of finding food or making a kill.

When they first emerge from their den at approximately 2 weeks old, young black-backed jackals are actually lead-grey in colour. Their characteristic coat markings will become apparent about 3 months later, by which time they will be hunting with their parents.

It is not uncommon for litter mates to pair up, and leave the family group when they are between 8 and 10 months old. This may have an impact on subsequent fertility, if in-breeding is occurring over many generations, and it may be that hunting pressures in South Africa have actually led directly to an increase in the numbers of jackals by breaking up such pairings, and forcing them to seek unrelated partners. Under normal circumstances, the tendency for in-breeding may help to exert a natural control on the number of jackals, relative to their food supply.

Changes in the black-backed jackal's environment in southern Africa have forced it into greater conflict with farmers. For example, the extinction of lions has reduced the potential for jackals to obtain their food by scavenging, and intensive hunting of antelope has depleted another of the jackal's food sources. Control of rodents, by means of poisons, and spraying to destroy insects has curbed the numbers of other natural prey species for the jackal.

Black-backed jackals are also trapped for their fur in some areas, and can be hunted throughout the year in South Africa outside protected areas. Even so, farmers are now advised only to kill those jackals known to be harming livestock, rather than attempting to wipe out as many as possible. They can be beneficial, with more than half their diet in the Giant's Castle Game Reserve, South Africa, being comprised of small mammals.

Various other hazards face black-backed jackals. Unwary pups are often seized close to their den by birds of prey, and large pythons appear to find these jackals easy prey, possibly because they stick to paths, where they can be easily ambushed.

Hunting may also be hazardous in some cases. Tribes of baboons (*Papio* spp.), for example, are quite capable of killing a jackal which attempts to snatch one of their young. Overall, it is unlikely that black-backed jackals survive for longer than 7 years in the wild, although they may live twice as long in captivity.

Simien jackal (Ethiopian jackal) *Canis simensis*

DISTRIBUTION
Confined to the plateaux area of the Simien, Arussi and Balé Mountains in Ethiopia, as well as north-eastern Shoa.

Relatively little is known about this mysterious and rare canid, which was originally called the Simien fox, although it is clearly a member of the genus *Canis*, and more closely allied to jackals rather than wolves in terms of its behaviour. Their coat is rufous in colour, with white underparts, and the tail has a black tip. The skull resembles that of other jackals, although the muzzle itself is noticeably elongated, and the teeth are quite small. They stand about 60 cm (23 in) at the shoulder, and males weigh about 18 kg (39 lb), with females slightly lighter.

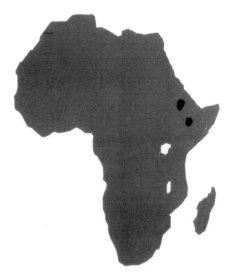

Distribution of the Simien jackal (*Canis simensis*).

Domestic dogs (*Canis familiaris*) pose a particular threat to the endangered Simien jackal (*Canis simensis*), by taking their prey, breeding with them and spreading disease.

Considered to be one of the most critically endangered canids in the world, the Simien jackal is restricted entirely to the mountains of Ethiopia, occurring at relatively high altitudes, typically above 3000 m (9843 ft), and up to nearly 5000 m (16,404 ft) above sea level. They are most commonly seen in areas of moorland, covered with low vegetation, where their coat coloration provides them with little camouflage. The surviving populations appear to be separate.

The majority of their food is lagomorphs and rodents, which are hunted largely during the daytime. The giant mole rat (*Tachyoryctes macrocephalus*) is a particularly important item in their diet. These jackals will often cache prey when such rodents are numerous. Local people claim that they also prey upon sheep, but there is little real evidence to substantiate this, although Simien jackals have been observed scavenging on the carcass of a cow, and hunting larger quarry such as reedbuck.

While these jackals tend to hunt alone, they are nevertheless quite social by nature, with groups coming together at various times during the day, and at dusk. Pairing and mating occur during the autumn and winter months, with pregnancy lasting about 9 weeks. The young, numbering up to seven, are born in a den, often located close to the base of cliffs or in level grassy areas. These typically have more than one entrance, and consist of a series of connecting tunnels. Helpers may be present, and assist with the rearing of the pups; a typical group is comprised of seven animals, in areas where the species is still reasonably numerous.

The largest population of Simien jackals is to be found in the Balé Mountains National Park, where an estimated 700 individuals survive. In the

143

Simien Mountains there were thought to be fewer than 20 of these jackals when a survey was carried out during 1976, just before this part of the country was sealed off by the authorities, and there is no current indication of their status today. This group was said to be nocturnal as a result of human persecution. The pelts are highly valued locally. In the Arussi region the population is in decline, now down to below 100 individuals, while the recently recorded group in north-eastern Shoa is thought to be small.

Simien jackals are protected by law in Ethiopia, and the bulk of their population is also within the boundaries of national parks, giving additional protection. Even so, enforcement of such legislation can be difficult, and hunting may be continuing. A study has recently been undertaken to gain more insight into this species, with a view to assisting its conservation.

It appears that overgrazing may affect the population of rodents on which the Simien jackals depend, and domestic dogs will also kill rats, competing with the jackals in some areas. Cross-breeding between these two species remains a risk factor, as does the introduction of disease by dogs into the relatively small areas where these jackals still occur. A further problem is that Simien jackals are surprisingly tame in some areas, approaching to within 3 m (10 ft) of people; this makes them very vulnerable to hunters.

Fennec fox *Fennecus zerda*

DISTRIBUTION
The desert area of North Africa, including Morocco, Algeria, Tunisia, Libya, Egypt and the Sudan. Also recorded on two occasions in the Middle East, from Kuwait and the Sinai, but precise information on populations here is lacking.

The fennec fox is the smallest of all the wild canids, measuring about 20 cm (8 in) at the shoulder and weighing between 1 and 1.5 kg (2–3 lb). They show the typical features associated with a desert species. Their coat is pale cream overall, often with darker coloration, ranging from fawn to grey, on the sides of the body, and a more solid line running along the spine. The tail is tipped with black, with the caudal gland at its base also marked by a darker area of fur.

The large ears of the fennec, which help it to hear effectively and assist with thermoregulation, can measure up to 15 cm (6 in) in length. They are dark on their outer surface, with white fur evident inside the pinnae. The fennec's dependence on its hearing is further reflected by the enlargement of the tympanic bullae of the skull, located beneath the ear openings.

The teeth are relatively small, the canines in particular being reduced in size. This is probably because large prey is not taken by these foxes. Even so, they have been known to kill animals bigger than themselves, such as rabbits. They naturally prey on small desert rodents, including gerbils, as well as lizards, and will dig for roots, which can provide a valuable source of moisture. Birds, insects and eggs are also eaten regularly when available. It is said that they climb date palms to obtain fruit, although this is probably an exaggeration. They are unlikely to be able to scale tall palms without low

The fennec fox (*Fennecus zerda*) has large ears which help to detect the calls of the desert-dwelling rodents on which this species often feeds.

branches for support, and are more likely to feed on fruit which has fallen to the ground.

Fennec foxes will drink at water holes in the desert, but also appear well-adapted to survive with a minimum intake of fluid. Their kidneys, like those of other desert animals, are able to restrict water loss from the body in the form of urine to a minimum.

Their burrowing activity may also trigger the formation of dew, which can be lapped up. Fennec foxes occupy a permanent den, which they dig themselves. They appear to be relatively social, living in family groups in some areas, although the core structure of such colonial living remains the breeding pair.

The female fennec is unusual amongst wild canids in that she can produce two litters in a year. If the first is lost, then she is likely to give birth again between 2½ and 3 months later. Mating tends to occur in captivity during January and February, with the young being born on average about 50 days later, although this period can apparently extend for as long as 63 days.

Litters consist of between 2 and 5 offspring, and females become aggressive at this stage, vigorously defending their den. The male fox does not cross the threshold, but provides food for the group. The young are weaned by 10 weeks, and will be mature by a year old.

There is considerable variation in temperature in the desert areas where these foxes are found. Their thick undercoat provides insulation during the cold nights, while their pale coats help to reflect heat, as well as serving to conceal their presence against the sandy background. The soles of their feet are covered in hair, so the pads are invisible. This gives insulation against the

145

Distribution of the fennec fox (*Fennecus zerda*).

burning desert sand, and also means they can run more easily over loose sand, without losing their grip.

Fennec foxes can move quite fast, and are able to jump distances of 1.2 m (4 ft) or more. While they may bark rather like a small dog, they also make a purring sound like a domestic cat at close quarters within a family group. If threatened however, fennecs will snarl. They have long been hunted in various parts of their range, although they pose no threat to people or their livestock. In some areas, it appears that these foxes may have declined in numbers as a consequence.

African wild dog (African or Cape hunting dog) *Lycaon pictus*

DISTRIBUTION
Areas of sub-Saharan Africa, especially southern-central and eastern parts.

This distinctive species used to have a much wider range, extending over almost the entire African continent, from the southern Sahara southwards and eastwards to Egypt. Today, their range at the tip of the continent is dramatically reduced, and they extend no further than the Sudan in the north.

A number of factors are responsible for this decline. The distribution of the ungulates which form the bulk of their prey has been curtailed, and African wild dogs have been heavily persecuted by people. They now tend to be confined largely to protected areas, where human contact is likely to be minimal.

The highly social nature of these canids has also contributed to their decline, in the face of hunting pressures. Studies carried out in Zimbabwe have shown that in some areas, populations have fallen to barely 1 per cent of

146

their former levels in just 5 years. The small numbers of African wild dogs in packs means that achieving and retaining kills becomes progressively more difficult. Pup mortality, which tends to be high in any event, also increases, with fewer helpers available to watch over and feed the youngsters.

The distinctive coloration of these wild dogs is highly individualistic, and may help group members to recognize each other. There is a longer area of hair extending from the underside of the throat back towards the chest. The tail is also bushy, and often ends in a white tip. Young African wild dogs are a combination of black and white at first, gaining yellowish-red markings as they mature, adding to their blotched appearance.

In terms of size, these are relatively large canids, measuring up to 78 cm (31 in) at the shoulder, and weighing 25 kg (55 lb) on average. Their ears are large, and strikingly rounded or oval in shape, with the muzzle being broad and short. A unique feature associated with this species is the absence of dew claws on the front feet. The legs themselves are relatively slender yet powerful, as suits a species that relies on pace as a critical component of its hunting abilities.

The prey taken by African wild dogs varies, according to the area concerned. In Hwange National Park, Zimbabwe for example, kudu (*Tragelaphus strepsiceros*) and impala (*Aepyceros melampus*) are their favoured quarry, while further north, in the Serengeti, wildebeest (*Connochaetes gnou*) and Thompson's gazelle (*Gazella thomsoni*) are taken.

All adult members of the pack will take part in a hunt, aside from those caring for the pups, with the average pack size today varying from about 6 to 15 individuals. This represents a dramatic decline from a century ago, when

African wild dogs (*Lycaon pictus*) have a well-defined social order.

Distribution of the African wild dog (*Lycaon pictus*).

there could be more than 100 African wild dogs living in a group, and up to 500 have been recorded. Today, packs of over 30 are exceedingly rare.

It is difficult to gain an accurate insight into the numbers of these canids however, because they are so nomadic. They may range over a huge area, from 500 km² (193 square miles), up to 1500 km² (579 square miles) or more, apart from the breeding period, when their pups are too small to travel long distances.

There is no doubting the tremendous fall in their numbers – a trend that appears to have accelerated in recent years. The latest estimates suggest that their entire population may now be as low as 2000 individuals, and the species has already disappeared or is very nearly extinct in 20 African countries. Elsewhere, the population of African wild dogs has almost halved in Zimbabwe, for example, in just a decade. Without effective protection, current projections suggest this species could be extinct in barely 20 years.

Many of the remaining populations may already be too fragmented and reduced in size to survive, although African wild dogs can live successfully in a variety of habitats, from open grassland to forested regions of Mount Kenya. Few other animals prove such effective hunters, with some packs achieving successful kills in nine out of every ten attempts.

Having targeted a particular individual, often because it is perceived to be weaker or slower, the pack will pursue it to the exclusion of all others. These dogs can run at speeds averaging 50 km per hour (31 mph) or more over long distances, and chase their quarry over several kilometres, before achieving a kill. The unfortunate animal is pulled to the ground and disembowelled, a manner of killing which has given the African wild dog a reputation as a vicious killer.

In fact, there is no sign of aggression following a kill. Pups feed before adults, and when they are too young to leave the den, members of the pack

Zimbabwe is just one country in Africa where the decline of the African wild dog (*Lycaon pictus*) has been particularly marked in recent years. These canids are unusual in that they often hunt in open grassland areas, with a high degree of success.

The tip of the tail of these canids is often white, and may be used for visual communication.

gulp down food, and return to the youngsters, regurgitating it for them. They swallow food quickly, before other predatory scavengers such as lions or hyaenas take over the kill.

On average, each dog consumes up to 5 kg (11 lb) of meat. Small packs need to kill more frequently, because their food is more likely to be stolen from them. African wild dogs appear able to go without drinking for days, but will do so regularly when water is available.

Packs hunt both morning and evening, seeking out shade where they can rest during the hottest part of the day. They locate their quarry by sight, but when food is in short supply, they will continue hunting after dark if necessary. There have been stories of African wild dogs attacking people, but there appears to be no real evidence to support such claims.

The structure of their packs is highly unusual. As mentioned previously (see page 66), they are comprised predominantly of males, which are likely to be related to each other, and at least one female from a different lineage. Only the dominant pair is likely to breed, with the mating season being very variable. Pups may be born virtually throughout the year as a consequence, even in the same area. Nevertheless, peaks of reproductive activity may be observed during the dry season, when game is concentrated around the remaining water holes, making it easier to hunt.

Female African wild dogs are prolific, and may have as many as 15 offspring in a single litter, although their average litter size is between 7 and 10 pups. Pregnancy lasts about 10 weeks on average, and generally, right from birth, males predominate, although the actual mechanism underlying this phenomenon is unclear.

The relatively high number of offspring can only be reared successfully by the co-operation of the other pack members, and gives some hope for the continued survival of the species in areas where adequate protection can be given. All will feed the pups, and remain close to the den, until the young are able to join with the pack and travel further afield, from the age of 3 months onwards. They will be able to hunt effectively by the time they are a year old.

Young females leave the group when they are between 18 months and 2½ years old. The male line with the pack may continue over numerous generations, however, lasting for a decade or more in some cases. Should disaster befall a breeding female, other members of the pack may manage to rear the cubs on their own. On one occasion males were observed to raise a litter of pups successfully from the age of 5 weeks old, when their mother died. In the wild, African wild dogs are unlikely to live for longer than 11 years, although handicapped individuals will be allowed to feed alongside other members of the pack, provided that they can keep up with the group.

While human persecution remains the main threat to the species, disease outbreaks can have serious effects in some localities. Distemper and cases of anthrax are regular hazards. A number of research projects are currently underway to give greater insight into the biology and habits of African wild dogs. A degree of in-breeding, which has led to eastern and southern groups becoming genetically distinct, is likely to become more of a problem, as the numbers of these dogs decline in the wild.

Profiling for this purpose is already underway. Satellite tracking is being used to monitor the movements of packs in and near the Kruger National

The unusually broad and rounded ear shape of the African wild dog (*Lycaon pictus*) is clearly evident here, as is its broad, powerful muzzle.

Park, while extensive work is being carried out in Botswana to discover the threat posed to livestock by these canids, helping to facilitate conservation planning for the future. Unfortunately, one of the problems is that African wild dogs are no respecters of park boundaries, frequently wandering into other areas where, in spite of theoretical protection, they are often shot.

Bat-eared fox (black-eared or Delande's fox) *Otocyon megalotis*

DISTRIBUTION

Occurs in two distinct populations: one in East Africa, extending from Somalia, Ethiopia and southern Sudan south to Tanzania, the other ranging from Angola and southern parts of Zambia down to the southern tip of the continent, although it is not found in all eastern areas.

It is likely that in the past, these foxes had a continuous distribution across Africa, but climatic changes influencing the availability of food, and human hunting pressures may have been responsible for splitting their population. They stand 30–40 cm (12–15 in) tall at the shoulder, and can vary in weight from 2 to 5 kg (4–11 lb).

Their body coloration is greyish-brown, with a prominent black stripe running down their tail, which terminates in a black tip. The most distinctive feature of this species is its ears, however, which can measure 13 cm (5 in) in length. This characteristic is also seen in other foxes found in relatively arid areas, such as the fennec (*Fennecus zerda*), and may serve a thermoregulatory function, dissipating heat from the body, as well as helping to pinpoint sounds.

The unusual dentition of bat-eared foxes (see page 32) is related directly to their diet, which has also influenced the surrounding musculature of the jaws.

Distribution of the bat-eared fox (*Otocyon megalotis*).

The bat-eared fox (*Otocyon megalotis*) is sometimes known as the black-eared fox, because of the dark tips to the ears. These can be clearly seen in this photograph.

These foxes are mainly insectivorous in their feeding habits, with termites comprising over half their food intake, according to various studies. Beetles of different types also feature prominently, while rodents and other vertebrates constitute less than 10 per cent. Their distribution can be closely correlated with *Hodotermes* termites, which is their favoured quarry.

In some areas, bat-eared foxes forage for food during the day, whereas in other parts of their range they are essentially nocturnal. The breeding period is also variable, although there is usually a strong pair bond established, which may last over a number of years, with the foxes rearing their offspring in the same den each year.

The gestation period averages around 10 weeks, with as many as six pups then being born. The male fox will watch over his offspring on occasions, leaving his mate free to forage on her own. By 6 months old, the youngsters are fully grown, and mature soon afterwards. The majority will disperse at this stage, but some females stay, forming a breeding group the following year.

There is safety in numbers for these relatively small foxes. They can then drive off potential predators such as leopards (*Panthera pardus*) and jackals. Perhaps because of this, bat-eared foxes do not show territorial instincts, although some scent-marking does occur. Their home ranges are frequently small and overlapping, typically varying from 0.24–1.5 km^2 (0.1–0.6 square miles).

Unfortunately, this means that disease can spread relatively easily within populations, causing widespread reduction in their numbers. This has been noted in various parts of their range, with rabies often being identified as the culprit.

This is one species that may benefit from an increase in the ranching of cattle though, because the resulting areas of open grassland provide additional habitat for their main prey – termites. The fur of bat-eared foxes is not of economic significance internationally, but is used in some areas, notably Botswana where the species was unknown until 1965. In spite of this hunting pressure, bat-eared foxes have become relatively common here since then.

Blanford's fox (Afghan or hoary fox) *Vulpes cana*

DISTRIBUTION
Traditionally regarded as being Afghanistan and south-western parts of the former USSR, as well as north-east Iran. Then described from Israel and Oman, and now believed to be more widely distributed through Arabia.

Relatively little is known about this small fox. It tends to occur in rocky hills, ranging up to an altitude of 2000 m (6562 ft), and may also be found in barren lowland areas as well, close to the Dead Sea for example. Blanford's fox stands about 30 cm (12 in) tall at the shoulder, and weighs between 1.5 and 3 kg (3–6½ lb).

Distribution of Blanford's fox (*Vulpes cana*), excluding Arabia where its status is currently unclear.

The ears of this species are large, as befits a desert-dwelling species, but the pads are not covered by fur. The tail is long, sometimes nearly doubling the fox's length when extended, and typically has a dark tip, although this may be white in some areas. Body coloration varies somewhat through the species' range, but there is generally a black stripe visible down the back, with the surrounding area of coat being brownish, becoming whiter on the underparts.

The snout of Blanford's fox is slender, and reports suggest that these foxes tend to eat more fruit than other species. In Baluchistan, they are known to eat ripe melons, as well as grapes and olives. Insects would also appear to be consumed regularly, and small mammals are caught on occasions.

In Israel, the mating period extends from December to January, with up to three pups being born about 8 weeks later. The young foxes are weaned after a further interval of 2 months, and can breed by 8 months old. They appear to lead a fairly solitary lifestyle, being active at night.

This species is relatively numerous in Israel where it is protected. Elsewhere through their range, Blanford's foxes are considered to be rare, and are heavily persecuted for their fur. Trapping is reputedly straightforward, since they show little fear, and so are easy to catch.

Cape fox (silver 'jackal'; kama fox) *Vulpes chama*

DISTRIBUTION
Southern Africa, to the south of the Zambezi River, and extending into central Namibia and south-western Angola, as well as Botswana further to the west.

Occurring in arid areas, the Cape fox is one of three *Vulpes* species present in Africa, but the only member of its genus to be encountered south of the Equator. Cape foxes inhabit veldt and savannah and avoid forested regions. Males stand approximately 36 cm (14 in) at the shoulder, and weigh about 2.5 kg (5 lb); the females are slightly lighter. They are silvery-grey in colour, with the head and upper portion of the forelimbs more reddish in tone.

Little has been recorded about their habits. Individuals hunt separately for food, seeking small rodents, rabbits and insects, as well as other items including reptiles, eggs, fruit, berries and seeds. They may also scavenge around human settlements, seeking edible refuse. Cape foxes are nocturnal, hiding during the day in a suitable den, either underground or in among rocks.

The mating period appears somewhat variable, proving seasonal only in some parts of their range. Pregnancy lasts just over 7 weeks, with 3–5 offspring forming a typical litter. They will begin hunting at 4 months old, and apparently soon split off after this stage, although it is not unknown for these foxes to share territory where food resources are adequate. They do not appear to form packs, however, even where they are numerous.

In some parts of their range, Cape foxes may be on the increase, but elsewhere they have been heavily persecuted, largely because of a widespread belief among farmers that they attack domestic stock, particularly sheep at lambing time. Such losses would appear to be greatly exaggerated, with the foxes scavenging on carcasses, rather than actively killing farmstock. As a

Distribution of the Cape fox (*Vulpes chama*).

result however, up to 5000 have been destroyed annually in the Orange Free State alone, where the total population is estimated not to exceed 31,000 individuals. A decline in the numbers of these foxes has been noted as a consequence during recent years, and there has been a concomitant increase in black-backed jackals (*Canis mesomelas*) here.

Pale fox (pallid or African sand fox) *Vulpes pallida*

DISTRIBUTION
The Sahel region bordering the Sahara, extending across Africa from Senegal in the west to Somalia in the east. Also present in the Sudan, occupying an area from east of the River Nile to the Red Sea.

One of the most mysterious members of the genus, in spite of its wide range, the pale fox most closely resembles the red fox in appearance, except that it is slightly smaller in size, and its legs and ears are somewhat larger. In terms of coloration, its coat may vary from buff to a pale shade of red. The tail is frequently a reddish-brown colour, and a dark stripe extends down the fox's back. The underparts, as well as the face and the inside of the ears are white. Pale foxes can weigh between 1.5 and 3 kg (3–6 lb), and stand about 25 cm (10 in) tall at the shoulder.

Their molar teeth are well-developed, with recent research suggesting that these foxes are mainly dependent on berries, fruit and vegetable matter for their food, although they will catch rodents and small birds on occasions, as well as lizards and other reptiles.

They prefer to hunt at night, in the open country where they occur. Pale foxes live in arid areas, but may also be encountered occasionally in more

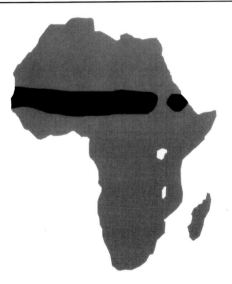

Distribution of the pale fox (*Vulpes pallida*).

wooded habitat. Little is known about their breeding habits in the wild, and there is no information on their current status, although they are not thought to be endangered.

Based on the sparse information that is available, it appears that these foxes are social by nature, living in communal burrows, which can form an intricate network of tunnels. These may extend back a distance of 15 m (49 ft), terminating in broader chambers lined with vegetation brought in, presumably as bedding by the foxes.

Rüppell's fox (sand fox) *Vulpes rueppelli*

DISTRIBUTION
Occurs further north than the preceding species, extending from Morocco in North Africa eastwards to Afghanistan and Pakistan. Also probably found across most of the Arabian peninsula.

Similar in height and weight to the pale fox (*V. pallida*), Rüppell's fox has a relatively slender body and large ears. Its coloration can vary markedly through its wide range, from buff to a more pronounced shade of grey. A rufous stripes runs down its back. The underparts are typically but not invariably paler, with a black area apparent on the facial area, extending from the eyes to the upper lip.

Pale foxes occur in desert areas, which may be either sandy or stony. Their pads are furred to protect them from reflected heat during the daytime. They live in pairs or family groups, but are less social than pale foxes. A pair may share a den together, tending to move to a new site within a

Distribution of Rüppell's fox (*Vulpes rueppelli*).

week. The size of their territory almost certainly varies somewhat, but can extend over 50 km^2 (19 square miles) in the case of a pair.

They are omnivorous in their feeding habits, eating both animal and vegetable matter readily, and they are not averse to scavenging at rubbish dumps to acquire food. Rüppell's foxes are essentially nocturnal in their habits, a fact reflected by the relatively large size of their whiskers.

The breeding period may be during the winter, but precise information is lacking about this at present. It is believed that two or three pups form the average litter, but virtually nothing else has been recorded about their development. Even their gestation period is currently unknown, although it is unlikely to differ significantly from that of other members of the genus.

There are also no population estimates, but this species is probably reasonably numerous in various parts of its range. It is not hunted extensively for its fur, although occasional individuals may be killed, essentially for food by local people.

Chapter 8
Canids of Southern Asia and Australia

Apart from the indigenous species of this region, two have been introduced to new localities here by human activities. The spread of the red fox (*Vulpes vulpes*) in Australia has already been discussed (see page 23), as has the introduction of the dingo (*Canis familiaris dingo*) to this continent. Other species which range into this part of the world, being present in Asia, are the golden jackal (*Canis aureus*) and the grey wolf (*Canis lupus*).

Considering the significance of the Bering land bridge in the history of canid evolution, it is perhaps surprising that there are not more species occurring naturally in this part of the world with its wide diversity of habitats. Nevertheless, apart from the dhole (*Cuon alpinus*), there are just three species of *Vulpes* fox inhabiting this region.

Dhole (Asiatic wild dog; whistling hunter) *Cuon alpinus*

DISTRIBUTION
Occurs over a vast area, encompassing much of central and eastern parts of Asia, from India to China, and south to Java.

Although it is the most widely distributed canid in this part of Asia, the dhole is in decline in many countries. During the late Pleistocene, around a million years ago, it ranged widely through Europe as well, having appeared to have evolved in the vicinity of present-day China. In Europe, northern dholes used to be larger than those occurring further south in the Mediterranean area, and this trend is still apparent elsewhere, within their extant range today. Males are significantly heavier than females, weighing up to 20 kg (44 lb), whereas females rarely exceed 13 kg (28 lb). They can vary in height at the shoulder from 42 to 55 cm (16–21 in).

Sometimes described rather misleadingly as the red dog, the dhole's coat coloration is variable and can range from shades of brownish-grey through to mahogany red. Even pale, sandy-coloured individuals have been noted in some areas. The hair on the back may be tipped with black, as is the tail, although in some cases this area may be white. A white patch in the vicinity of the throat is common, and may extend down to the chest, and even reach the abdomen. Their ears are rounded, like those of the African wild dog (*Lycaon pictus*) and also have white hair evident on the periphery.

The more intense reddish coloration tends to occur in southern populations, while further north their coats are longer and dense, with a woolly undercoat which helps to protect against the cold. Dholes have a short, square-shaped muzzle that enables them to exert powerful pressure with their jaws. Their dental formula is unique within the Canidae; they have only two molars in each lower jaw, compared with three in other species. This means that they only have 40 teeth.

Living in packs, dholes hunt a variety of relatively large prey. In Siberia, they pursue reindeer (*Rangifer tarandus*), while in Tibet, they will catch wild sheep (*Ovis* spp.). The most detailed studies on their feeding habits have been carried out in India, where chital (*Axis axis*), a small deer, was found to be their major prey species, comprising almost three-quarters of their diet, followed by sambar (*Cervus unicolor*). They will also catch various rodents and lagomorphs, but pay little attention to farmstock, even where such animals are roaming free.

A pack will run down a large target animal using a technique similar to that employed by the African wild dogs, and kill it by means of evisceration. The dholes will then defend their kill resolutely against other predators, and have even been observed killing tigers (*Panthera tigris*) and bears (*Ursus* spp.) on occasions. If outnumbered, by a herd of wild pigs (*Suis* spp.), for example, they may decide to withdraw for a period however, until the pigs move on.

While they have gained a reputation for vicious behaviour, which stems largely from their killing method, dholes present no danger to people. When food is short, they may occasionally feed on carrion, while individuals will concentrate their efforts on hunting small animals during the dry season in India, where larger quarry is harder to find. Dholes will also eat some vegetable matter and fruit, as well as insects.

Dholes are not an easy species to study, but it appears that a typical pack is composed of between 5 and 12 individuals, the majority of whom are related to each other. Packs may come together and form larger units, described as

The dhole (*Cuon alpinus*) is another wild canid living and hunting in family groups, whose distribution has been significantly reduced in recent years.

Distribution of the dhole (*Cuon alpinus*).

clans, at least on a temporary basis outside the breeding period. Up to 40, and possibly as many as a 100 individuals may associate in this way. The clans then split up at the start of the mating period. In most groups there are twice as many males as females.

There is a dominance order established within the pack, but outbreaks of fighting are not common, and usually involve sub-adults. Their home range is strongly influenced by the availability of food and water, and averages about 40 km² (15 square miles), becoming smaller when there are pups. The breeding period is influenced by the area, although females can come into heat over a relatively broad period of time, from September to February in central and southern parts of northern India.

The young are born after a period of about 63 days in an underground den, which may have previously been occupied by a porcupine (*Hystrix* spp). A typical litter will comprise about four pups, but as many as ten have been known. Female dholes are social even when breeding, and may share a den at this stage, to rear their pups.

All members of the pack provide food for the youngsters, regurgitating this on demand. Some also guard the den while the remainder of the group are away hunting. The pups do not leave this area until they are at least 10 weeks old, and then squabble with each other to reinforce their order of dominance. This phase is largely over by the time that they start hunting with the pack, at approximately 7 months of age. Young dholes are mature by a year old, but it is not known when they leave their natal pack.

The reasons for the apparent decline in the numbers of dholes through

161

Tethered farmstock could present an easy target for a pack of dholes, but the available evidence suggests that these canids prefer their natural prey.

many parts of their range are hard to determine, since they tend not to be heavily persecuted, and avoid contact with people. In some areas, poisoning has been claimed as a factor, with dholes taking bait left for wolves (*Canis lupus*). The significance of this risk is unclear, however, since dholes do not display a great tendency to scavenge. In India, outbreaks of disease may curb their numbers, with both distemper and rabies being endemic here.

Dholes are known to fall victim to these infections, and this could account for the fact that only one pack is now said to remain within the Chitawin National Park. Elsewhere in India, populations have declined, to the point of extinction in some cases, particularly in the east of the country, although dholes still remain numerous in some areas, such as the Garo Hills of Meghalaya.

Their status in Thailand is unclear, although they are still thought to be reasonably common in Burma. A serious decline in their numbers has taken place in the former USSR, while in China, dholes are also scarce.

Dingo *Canis familiaris dingo*

DISTRIBUTION
Traditionally recognized from Australia, where it occurs in central areas, and down the eastern coast. Not present in Tasmania.

There is currently debate as to whether some of the dingo-like dogs found in Asia should be grouped with *Canis familiaris dingo*, although they are invariably smaller in size. Australian dingoes also show considerable diversity, in terms of both their height, which can vary from 40 to over 65 cm (15–25 in) at the shoulder, and their weight, with large male dingoes weighing 22 kg (48 lb) or possibly more in the eastern part of their range. This variance is to be expected, as they are not a pure species, although they could evolve along these lines.

This is becoming increasingly less likely however, as time passes. First introduced to Australia perhaps 4000 years ago (see page 88), dingoes have been persecuted ever since European settlers arrived, for killing sheep. Bounties are still paid on dead dingoes. Perhaps worse, however, from the dingo's standpoint, was the introduction of domestic dogs (*Canis familiaris familiaris*) in 1788, because cross-breeding has since become widespread. In south-eastern Australia, about one-third of the dingo population consists of hybrids.

True dingoes can be recognized by their teeth – the canines and carnassials are larger than those of either the domestic dog or hybrids – and by the fact that they only breed once a year, whereas most domestic dogs have two periods of heat annually.

Dingoes are highly adaptable in their feeding habits, catching or eating whatever is available in a given area, although they tend to prey mainly on macropod marsupials, such as kangaroos and wallabies. They occupy a wide range of habitats, including the arid interior of Australia, as well as the rainforest region of the Cape York peninsula.

In some areas, dingoes associate in groups, like their original ancestor the grey wolf (*Canis lupus*). Only the dominant female will breed; should other females mate successfully and give birth, she will almost invariably kill the

The dingo (*Canis familiaris dingo*) leads a solitary lifestyle, and has been heavily hunted in Australia, where it was thought to have been introduced as recently as 4000 years ago by early settlers.

Dingoes (*Canis familiaris dingo*), (left) have cross-bred extensively with domestic dogs in recent years, particularly in the south-east of Australia.

The New Guinea singing dog is a dingo-like canid which some would classify with the dingo. There is a marked lack of standardization in the size and coloration of this group of canids, in any event.

Distribution of the dingo
(*Canis familiaris dingo*).

puppies. Mating takes place between March and April, and up to ten pups may be born after a period of 63 days, although half this number is more usual. They will be fully independent from 6 months of age, but it may be 2 years before they start to breed.

The coloration of dingoes is relatively consistent, being a shade of ginger, which can range from a pale hue to a reddish hue. White areas of variable size are often present on the chest, and may also be evident elsewhere on the body, notably on the feet and the tip of the tail. In spite of continuing heavy persecution in some areas, dingoes remain surprisingly common, although they are shy by nature and rarely seen, particularly during the daytime. The only successful way of restricting their spread has been the construction of special dingo fences in sheep-grazing areas of western and eastern Australia.

Bengal fox (Indian fox) *Vulpes bengalensis*

DISTRIBUTION
Occurs in India, Nepal and Pakistan.

As in other species, males of the Bengal fox are larger and heavier than females. Relatively little is known about their behaviour, but they are thought to live in pairs. Although absent from densely forested areas, they can be observed in the foothills of the Himalayas, up to an altitude of 1500 m (4921 ft), living in burrows.

Distribution of the Bengal fox (*Vulpes bengalensis*).

Here these foxes are more numerous than in open areas of country, where they tend to be persecuted. Bengal foxes cause no damage to farmstock, and are simply killed for sport, although their body is reputed to have medicinal properties if eaten. In areas where they are subject to hunting pressures, these foxes have become mainly nocturnal. They feed on a wide variety of items, with invertebrates figuring prominently in their diet. They also catch rodents and the more terrestrial species of birds. Members of a pair usually hunt individually.

Almost nothing is known about the breeding habits of Bengal foxes, however, except that the gestation period lasts about 53 days, and four pups form a typical litter. Some pairs may be assisted by helpers. Whereas some dens used by this species take the form of a simple underground tunnel, others are far more complex, with a number of entrances, but the significance of these different dens is unclear at present.

Recognizable by its buff coat, with paler underparts and a black tip to its tail, the Bengal fox occurs at a relatively low density, with probably fewer than one individual per 10 km^2 (4 square miles) in suitable habitat. In some parts of their range, notably the Tirunelveli District of Tamil Nadu, these foxes are trapped as a source of food by nomads. Here a number are also killed by dogs each year. Overall however, this species does not appear to be under threat.

Corsac fox (Steppe fox) *Vulpes corsac*

DISTRIBUTION
Present in the south-eastern area of the former USSR, and over a wide area of central Asia. Also found in Afghanistan, Turkestan, plus Transbaikalia, northern Manchuria and Mongolia.

A typical member of the genus, the corsac fox is slightly smaller than the red fox (*Vulpes vulpes*). It is predominantly grey in coloration with yellower tones and a white chin, and inhabits semi-desert and steppeland areas through its range, although they will move into forested parts if food becomes scarce.

From the limited information available, it appears that corsac foxes favour rodents as the main item in their diet, although they also consume large quantities of insects. The teeth are relatively small and it is probable that they catch rodents using a characteristic style similar to that adopted by the red fox (*Vulpes vulpes*), leaping up into the air, and then dropping down on the prey, reducing its chances of escape. Their relatively large, broad ears are triangular in shape, and help them to locate the slightest rustle that could indicate the presence of a rodent.

The density of these foxes can be quite high in some areas, giving rise to the description of 'corsac cities', where there are numerous burrows adjoining each other. Unfortunately, human persecution appears to have eliminated

Distribution of the corsac fox (*Vulpes corsac*).

many groupings on such a scale, as these foxes are hunted for their fur, particularly in the former USSR, although this is not as valued as that from the red fox.

Corsac foxes often take over burrows dug by other animals such as marmots (*Marmota* spp.), and it is thought that they are more sociable by nature than other *Vulpes* species. They have been observed hunting in small groups, and living in close proximity to each other, although it may well be that these were related animals, probably a breeding pair with their offspring.

Mating occurs at the start of the year, and pregnancy lasts about 8 weeks on average. Typically, between two and six offspring are born, but up to 11 in a single litter have been documented. The male probably assists with the rearing of the young but this is not known with certainty.

The number of corsac foxes appears to show a cyclical variation to some extent, which may be linked to the rodent population that forms the basis of their diet. It seems apparent that they will migrate when food is short in a particular area, and they also have caches in more plentiful periods. Little is known about their precise numbers, but it does seem that increased ploughing of land for agricultural purposes has reduced the population of these foxes in some areas.

Hunting pressures may have made them more nocturnal in parts as well, although they are said to tame readily, and lack the pungent odour associated with their close relative, the red fox. In fact, in the seventeenth century they were popular pets in the former USSR.

Tibetan fox (Tibetan sand fox) *Vulpes ferrilata*

DISTRIBUTION
Restricted to Tibet, the Sutlej Valley in the far north-west of India and northern Nepal, occurring here in the Mustang district.

Little is known about these small, upland foxes. They have a particularly elongated snout, and it is thought that their diet is composed largely of rodents. In terms of coloration, Tibetan foxes are a shade of rusty yellow on their upperparts, becoming greyer on the sides of their bodies, with the chin and chest frequently white. A study of the anatomy of their skull reveals that their teeth are well-developed, particularly the canines, which are sharp and elongated. Their hearing is also thought to be acute, which probably assists them to locate prey.

Tibetan foxes can be found at altitudes of about 5000 m (16,400 ft) on the mountain plateaux that are their home. Here they den in burrows concealed under large rocks, or retreat into piles of boulders. The fur is dense to protect them from the bitter cold in this region during the winter, and the ears are relatively small.

Little else has been recorded about this species. Pairs may be seen hunting together in some areas, and mating takes place towards the end of February. A litter of between two and five pups is then born up to 2 months later.

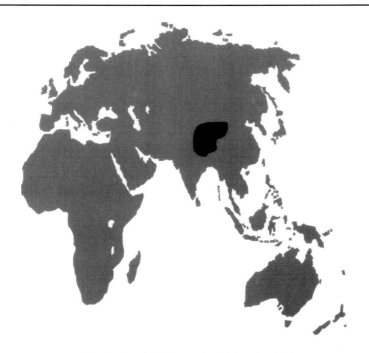

Distribution of the Tibetan fox (*Vulpes ferrilata*).

Although considered to be widely distributed through their range, these foxes are not particularly common close to human settlements. Trapping in these areas has affected their numbers here, with their pelts being made into hats in Tibet.

169

Chapter 9
Canids of South America

There are ten species of wild canid occurring in South America today, and only one of these – the grey fox (*Urocyon cinereoargenteus*) is represented further north, which is its main centre of distribution. A further species, the Falkland Island 'wolf' (*Dusicyon australis*) used to have a restricted distribution on these islands off the coast of South America, but was exterminated in the late 1800s.

Although often described as foxes, there is a growing tendency to use the Spanish name 'zorro', to indicate that these canids are unrelated to the true *Vulpes* foxes. Relatively little is known about the biology of a number of these species, and they are rarely seen alive outside South America, although some zorros are widely trapped for the international fur trade.

Maned wolf *Chrysocyon brachyurus*

DISTRIBUTION
Eastern South America, occurring in parts of Bolivia, Brazil, Argentina and Uruguay.

One of the most distinctive of all canids, the maned wolf is actually more closely related to foxes than wolves. Its long, slender legs give it the appearance of walking on stilts, and individuals can measure as much as 76 cm (29 in) at the shoulder. The ears are large, and the reddish fur is relatively long. The legs, as well as the muzzle, are usually blackish in coloration. Maned wolves weigh just over 20 kg (44 lb) on average.

Secretive by nature, maned wolves are solitary and hard to observe. They occur in fairly open country, ranging from grassland plains to the borders of forests and they may even be found in swampy areas, close to rivers. Clearance of woodland in some areas may be helping this species to expand its range, but this also tends to bring increased risk of human persecution.

Maned wolves occupy large areas of territory, with pairs sharing a suitable region, although they do not hunt together on a regular basis. Domestic chickens are a favoured item in their diet, which clearly brings them into conflict with farmers. They rarely prey upon other domestic animals, however, preferring instead to hunt small rodents and other birds. Vegetable matter and fruit also feature prominently in their diet.

The legs of the maned wolf are not well-adapted for digging, and it may actually use its teeth to unearth rodents from their burrows. Probably for this reason as well, the den is often located above ground, frequently in a crevice under rocks. Young may even be born in dense vegetation. The mating season of this species extends from December through to June, peaking towards the end of this period. The female remains in oestrus for just 5 days, however, and

Pairs of maned wolves (*Chrysocyon brachyurus*) may share a territory, but spend little time in each other's company outside the breeding period.

The slim physique of the maned wolf (*Chrysocyon brachyurus*) is clearly seen here.
Agility is important, as this wild canid feeds mainly on small prey, including domestic
poultry. It is sometimes persecuted by farmers as a result.

mating typically lasts around 10 minutes. She will give birth to a relatively
small number of offspring – typically around three – about 65 days later.

Young maned wolves are a darker, greyish shade at birth, and appear to be
relatively short-legged. Both parents participate actively in the rearing of their
cubs, one member of the pair remaining with them at all times, while the other
presumably hunts for food. The youngsters themselves are unlikely to breed
until their second year. Certainly in captivity, they may be fed by their father
regurgitating food until they are 10 months old, but little is known about their
dispersal in the wild.

Although the pelt of the maned wolf is not of commercial value, these canids
are still hunted by farmers, fearful of damage to their livestock. Education
programmes are now being undertaken in some areas to dissuade farmers
from this approach. This distinctive species is currently considered to be
vulnerable, with disease playing a part in its decline.

In both Bolivia and Uruguay, maned wolves are believed to be either
extinct, or surviving only in very low numbers. Within Argentina there could
be 1500, based on estimates carried out during the 1970s, when the species
was then common in Formosa province. Current information on its status is
presently scarce, but research is also currently underway here. In Brazil,
however, maned wolves appear to have increased in numbers during the past
decade, at least in Serra da Canastra, where grassland areas have been
extended.

Distribution of the maned wolf (*Chrysocyon brachyurus*).

It seems that the maned wolf, with its highly individual appearance, has an evolutionary history dating back over 6 million years, to the time that many large canids became extinct on the South American continent. It is not closely related to any other canid found in this region today.

Crab-eating zorro (crab-eating fox) *Cerdocyon thous*

DISTRIBUTION
Ranges through northern South America from Colombia and Venezuela down to Brazil; largely absent from the interior until further south, being found here in Bolivia, Paraguay, Uruguay and northern Argentina.

This widely distributed canid tends to be encountered in relatively open country, being absent from the rainforest region of the Amazon Basin. It is greyish-brown in colour, becoming more rufous on the legs, ears and face. The tip of the tail is black, as are the tips of the ears, although there can be noticeable variation between individuals from different parts of their range.

The word '*thous*' in their scientific name is the Greek for 'jackal', and it is true that these zorros resemble members of this group to some extent. They are relatively bold and highly opportunistic in their feeding habits, eating almost anything that is edible and adjusting their feeding habits according to the season. When hunting, they restrict themselves to smaller rodents and other creatures of similar size, such as frogs and lizards. Land crabs are also frequently consumed, along with the eggs of turtles, and these foxes will scavenge for food as well. They also eat vegetable matter, including cultivated fruits such as banana on occasions.

Like the golden jackal (*Canis aureus*), this species may not display a regular reproductive cycle. Females can come into heat at any stage of the year, a phenomenon described as aseasonal oestrus. Some may have two such periods annually. Close to the equator, the breeding season is not closely defined, but it tends to become more restricted further south.

Pregnancy lasts on average around 53 days, with between three and six pups forming a typical litter. These are likely to be born in a den taken over from another species; crab-eating zorros appear reluctant to dig their own dens. The young separate from their parents by the time they reach 8 months of age, and females will breed from a year onwards.

Nocturnal by nature, these foxes may be shot for their pelts, although these are of little value. They are regarded as common throughout most of their range. Crab-eating foxes do not appear to maintain strong territorial boundaries and occur mainly in pairs, accompanied by youngsters. In Brazil, larger groups may form, comprised of a pair and their adult offspring, as well as younger pups.

Distribution of the crab-eating zorro (*Cerdocyon thous*).

Land crabs may feature in the diet of the crab-eating zorro (*Cerdocyon thous*), but a wide range of other prey is also taken.

Seasonal movements have been detected in some areas, with the foxes retreating to higher ground during the wet season. Here they feed increasingly on invertebrates, as well as fruit. They return to lower levels for the rest of the year, when it seems that small mammals figure more prominently in their diet, as well as the land crabs, although there is no evidence to show that these are a particularly favoured item.

Culpeo *Dusicyon culpaeus*

DISTRIBUTION
Extends down almost the entire length of the western side of South America, occurring in Ecuador, Peru, Bolivia, Argentina and Chile. May also extend into Colombia.

The size of these foxes increases in a southerly direction, and they are the largest member of their genus, with their weight ranging from 5 to 13.5 kg (11–29 lb). In terms of coloration, their heads and legs are tawny, becoming paler under the chin, while the back and sides of the body are greyish, and the tail has a black tip.

Rodents and lagomorphs are their major prey, although in some areas, they also attack sheep. Studies suggest that culpeos tend to take lambs which are more than a week old, and may account for up to 7 per cent of the total number born in some areas. Nevertheless, they are beneficial in that they catch many rabbits, which were introduced to this part of South America in about 1915.

Distribution of the culpeo (*Dusicyon culpaeus*).

These additional sources of prey may have facilitated the spread of the culpeo, from the foothills of the Andes where it used to occur out across the Patagonian plain. They can be found up to an altitude of 4500 m (14,760 ft) in some areas.

Relatively little is known about the social life of these foxes. The mating period extends between August and October. The female chooses a den concealed in rocks or hidden in vegetation, and gives birth to five cubs on average, after a gestation period lasting about 2 months.

Their life expectancy would appear to be short – a Chilean study found that just five out of every 100 foxes were over 2 years old. Investigations in Argentina revealed that there was an imbalance in the sex ratio of the population in Neuquén province, with approximately six males to every four females, but the cause and significance of this situation is unclear.

Within Argentina, the culpeo is most numerous in the southern part of the country. The population of 200,000 in Patagonia remained constant during a 6-year study, but in Salta province, in northern Argentina, these foxes are thought to be on the verge of extinction.

In Peru, culpeos are most numerous in the southern highlands of the country, although they are not encountered in the coastal forest region. Their numbers in Chile are unlikely to be high, but they do extend right to the tip of the continent here, being present on Tierra del Fuego and Isla Hoste, part of the Cape Horn Archipelago. There is little current information from elsewhere on the culpeo's status. Although it appears that only Argentina has exported skins in recent years, it is almost certainly hunted for this reason in other countries such as Bolivia.

Grey zorro (South American grey fox; chilla) *Dusicyon griseus*

DISTRIBUTION
Southern South America, present in Chile and Argentina. May range into Peru.

One of the smallest members of the *Dusicyon* genus, the grey zorro stands about 40 cm (15 in) tall at the shoulder, and weighs around 4 kg (9 lb). As its name suggests, it is predominantly grey, with rust-coloured markings on the head, and large ears.

Rodents tend to form the most important item in the diet of these foxes, although they will eat more berries in the autumn. They appear not to prey actively upon sheep, although they may eat carrion. Breeding details are similar to those of the preceding species, but overall, probably less is documented about their lifestyle.

What is clear, however, is that this species has been very heavily trapped for its fur, with this trade involving more than a million pelts in the early 1980s.

Distribution of the grey zorro (*Dusicyon griseus*). The dark tone indicates main distribution; the mid-grey tone indicates possible isolated population.

Argentina has been the source of many of these skins, but the population, at least in the Rio Negro area of Patagonia appears to be relatively constant, in spite of this severe hunting pressure.

Heavy snowfalls do depress the population, presumably with many foxes dying of starvation as a consequence, but even so, their numbers soon recover. Nevertheless, increasing competition with the culpeo (*D. culpaeus*) may have a more severe effect on their numbers in the future in this region.

In Chile, the grey zorro is generally considered to be scarce, and is supposedly protected by law, although this does not apparently prevent trapping. The southern part of Chile seems to be where this species remains most numerous at present.

Azara's zorro (pampas fox) *Dusicyon gymnocercus*

DISTRIBUTION
Central South America, found with certainty in northern Argentina, south-east Brazil, Paraguay and Uruguay.

Present in a wide range of habitats from deserts through to open forest, these foxes tend to be most common in lowland prairie areas, up to an altitude of 1000 m (3280 ft), although they have been recorded as high as 4000 m (13,120 ft) above sea level. Azara's zorro is a medium-sized member of the genus, with a grey back and sides offset against white underparts and paws, and a rufous head.

They appear to lead a relatively solitary lifestyle, feeding mainly on animals such as rodents and lagomorphs, but also catching birds. These foxes are said to attack lambs, and are hunted for this reason, as well as for their fur. Leg-hold traps are frequently used, along with poison if the purpose is simply to eliminate them. Even so, Azara's zorros do not display a great fear of people, and may simply freeze if threatened, rather than attempting to run off. They are often hunted on horseback. Smuggling of skins has been a problem, with enforcement having been reputedly lax in Paraguay in particular.

The mating period can extend from July to October, with the male bringing food to the den at first for his mate and family. Three to five pups form a typical litter and are born up to 60 days after mating. They will start hunting with their parents by the time they are about 3 months old. In some parts of its range, this species appears to have declined, largely because of hunting pressures, but elsewhere, in central Argentina, for example, it is still quite numerous.

Small-eared zorro *Dusicyon microtis*

DISTRIBUTION
Thought to range through the Amazon basin in northern South America. Recorded from parts of Brazil, Bolivia, Peru, Ecuador and Colombia, and may also occur in Venezuela.

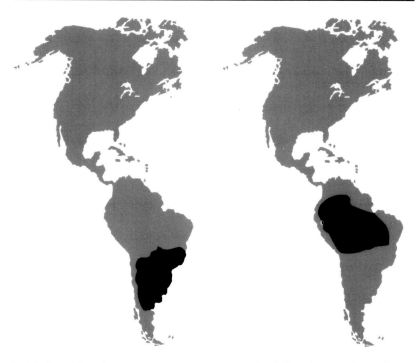

Distribution of Azara's zorro
(*Dusicyon gymnocercus*).

Distribution of the small-eared zorro
(*Dusicyon microtis*).

One of the most mysterious of all wild canids, virtually nothing is known about the small-eared zorro, in spite of its relatively wide area of distribution. It typically measures about 35 cm (14 in) at the shoulder, and weighs around 10 kg (22 lb). It appears to be nocturnal in its habits, according to native reports, and has been seen in rainforest up to an altitude of 1000 m (3280 ft). These zorros are considered to be rare throughout their range, which is itself not precisely defined as yet.

Sechuran zorro (Sechura fox) *Dusicyon sechurae*

DISTRIBUTION
Restricted to southern Ecuador and the adjoining northern area of Peru.

Another poorly studied species, the Sechuran zorro is an inhabitant of low grasslands and semi-desert in the coastal region where it occurs. It is named after the Sechura Desert, and is the smallest number of the genus, weighing little more than 3 kg (6½ lb). Its coloration is similar to that of the grey zorro (*D. griseus*), with pale creamy-fawn underparts.

In some areas, particularly during the winter, these zorros are forced to feed mainly on seed pods and beetles, although at other times they will catch

179

rodents and birds on occasions, as well as scavenging along the shoreline. They seem to be able to survive without access to drinking water, possibly by lapping at condensation.

Daytime is spent in a den, from which they emerge at night to hunt. Almost nothing is known about their social interactions or breeding behaviour, although young are said to be born in October. Sechuran zorros do not appear to be threatened by hunting pressures, but there is no available estimate of their population.

Hoary zorro (small-toothed dog) *Dusicyon vetulus*

DISTRIBUTION
Restricted to Minas Gerais and Matto Grosso in the south-western part of Brazil.

These zorros are again predominantly grey in colour, with pale underparts and a rufous tinge on the outer side of their legs and ears. Small in size, they weigh up to 4 kg (9 lb), and are found in mountain areas, where there are open areas of woodland and grassy savanna. Mainly active during the daytime, they prey on a variety of rodents and other small animals, as well as

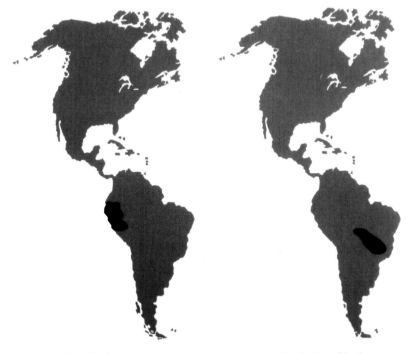

Distribution of the Sechuran zorro
(*Dusicyon sechurae*).

Distribution of the hoary zorro
(*Dusicyon vetulus*).

termites and grasshoppers. Their reputation for killing poultry has brought them into conflict with people. Little is known about their status, except that their numbers may vary in some areas through the year. They do not appear to be especially numerous overall.

Females will use old armadillo burrows as dens, giving birth here to as many as four offspring, typically in September. The role played by the male at this stage, and the subsequent dispersal of their offspring, is unknown.

Falkland Island wolf (Antarctic wolf; warrah) *Dusicyon australis*

DISTRIBUTION
Formerly occurred on West and East Falkland Islands, off the coast of Argentina.

This species stood about 60 cm (24 in) tall at the shoulder, and had brownish-grey upperparts, with black ears and pale underparts, while its bushy tail was tipped with white fur. It resembled a wolf in appearance, but had shorter legs. Its large skull had a broad muzzle, but its ears were small.

How these canids reached the Falkland Islands is unclear; it may be that their ancestors crossed on an ice sheet from the mainland during the Pleistocene epoch, around 1 million years ago, or alternatively, early South American settlers may have introduced dogs to the islands, where they subsequently evolved in isolation. Certainly, the records of this species describe it as being exceptionally tame, even when it was being heavily persecuted.

The first description of the Falkland Island wolf came from a British sailor serving on HMS *Welfare*, which visited the islands about 1689. The crew took a young pup of this species on board. It apparently lived quite happily within the confines of the ship for some months, until an engagement took place with a French warship, at which point, it leapt overboard.

Subsequent visitors to the Falkland Islands noted how these wild dogs would approach boats as they landed, apparently out of curiosity. They were said to bark like domestic dogs.

Before the arrival of domestic stock, these canids presumably scavenged along the shore, and ate penguins and other birds, as well as vegetation. They were the only mammalian predator on the islands and so prey were easy to come by. The introduction of cattle to the Falklands heralded the start of their decline. Spanish settlers killed them easily in large numbers, sticking them with knives having lured them to feed on a piece of meat offered in the other hand. Sheep farmers laid poisoned baits as well, although it is hard to assess the potential threat posed by these canids to their stock.

The naturalist Charles Darwin foresaw the extinction of this species when he visited the Falkland Islands in the *Beagle* in 1833. Worse followed, when the warrah, as it was known to the local people, attracted an official government bounty in 1839. Fur trappers then sought the species for its thick, dense fur. This was in demand in the fashion industry for a period, with large numbers of pelts being sent to New York.

One live warrah reached England in 1868, and lived for a number of years at London Zoo. The last known individual in the wild was killed at Shallow Bay, in the Hill Cove Canyon, in 1876, just 43 years after Darwin's visit. All that remains of this unique canid today is 11 specimens, some of them incomplete, scattered in museums around the world.

Bush dog (vinegar dog) *Speothos venaticus*

DISTRIBUTION
Ranges from Panama in Central America southwards through northern South America, where the species is present in Colombia, Venezuela, the Guyanas and Brazil, extending to north-eastern Argentina, Paraguay, and the eastern parts of Bolivia and Peru.

The unusual appearance of this species makes it one of the most distinctive of all canids. It is dark brown in colour, with small ears and a short tail. In contrast to the normal canid pattern, the underparts tend to be darker in coloration than the rest of their body. Bush dogs stand about 30 cm (12 in) tall at the shoulder, and are typically about twice as long, excluding their tail.

The fact that they are somewhat reminiscent of otters in appearance is not entirely coincidental. Active during the day, bush dogs live in groups and

Former distribution of the Falkland
Island wolf (*Dusicyon australis*).

Distribution of the bush dog
(*Speothos venaticus*).

Bush dogs (*Speothos venaticus*) are unusual among wild canids in that they tend to be most active during the daytime.

spend much of their time in water, being strong swimmers. Here they will hunt large water rodents, such as the paca (*Agouti paca*) and capybaras (*Hydrochaeris hydrochaeris*).

Little else is known about them. It is believed that females may have two periods of heat each year, and a tie may not necessarily occur during mating in this species. Bush dogs will excavate their own dens, although they will also often take over those dug by other species such as armadillos (*Peludos* spp.). Their young are thought to be born after a period of at least 2 months, with between four and six offspring forming a typical litter.

Bush dogs are generally considered to be rare through their range, but they face no obvious threats, aside from perhaps changes in habitat. They are not hunted for their fur, although young are sometimes reared as pets by the native Indians. These are said to behave rather like domestic dogs, readily rolling over to have their underparts tickled. The call of the bush dog is high-pitched and loud, and they can bark as well as squeal.

Checklist of Species

Taxonomic changes do occur from time to time, and there is no universal agreement about the classification of the Canidae, especially with regard to subspecies. The use of common names is also a vexed area, with fewer rules applying than in the case of scientific nomenclature. Both the scientific and common names used in this book are based on the system proposed by the IUCN/SSC Canid Specialist Group and the IUCN/SSC Wolf Specialist Group (see Ginsberg and Macdonald, 1990).

Arctic fox
Alopex lagopus lagopus
Alopex lagopus beringensis
Alopex lagopus fuliginosus
Alopex lagopus groenlandicus
Alopex lagopus hallensis
Alopex lagopus pribilofensis
Alopex lagopus sibiricus
Alopex lagopus spitzbergensis
Alopex lagopus ungava

Side-striped jackal
Canis adustus adustus
Canis adustus bweha
Canis adustus centralis
Canis adustus kaffensis
Canis adustus lateralis

Golden jackal
Canis aureus aureus
Canis aureus algirensis
Canis aureus anthus
Canis aureus bea
Canis aureus lupaster
Canis aureus maroccanus
Canis aureus riparius
Canis aureus soudanicus

Dingo
Canis familiaris dingo

Coyote
Canis latrans latrans
Canis latrans cagottis
Canis latrans clepticus
Canis latrans dickeyi
Canis latrans frustor
Canis latrans goldmani
Canis latrans hondurensis
Canis latrans impavidus
Canis latrans incolatus
Canis latrans jamesi
Canis latrans lestes
Canis latrans mearnsi
Canis latrans microdon
Canis latrans ochropus
Canis latrans peninsulae
Canis latrans texensis
Canis latrans thamnos
Canis latrans umpquensis
Canis latrans vigilis

Grey wolf
Canis lupus lupus
Canis lupus albus
Canis lupus alces
Canis lupus arabs
Canis lupus arctos
Canis lupus baileyi
Canis lupus bernardi
Canis lupus campestris
Canis lupus chanco

Grey wolf (*continued*)
Canis lupus columbianus
Canis lupus crassodon
Canis lupus fuscus
Canis lupus griseoalbus
Canis lupus hudsonicus
Canis lupus irremotus
Canis lupus labradorius
Canis lupus ligoni
Canis lupus lycaon
Canis lupus mackenzii
Canis lupus nubilus
Canis lupus occidentalis
Canis lupus orion
Canis lupus pallipes
Canis lupus pambasileus
Canis lupus signatus
Canis lupus tundrarium

Black-backed jackal
Canis mesomelas mesomelas
Canis mesomelas achrotes
Canis mesomelas arenarum
Canis mesomelas elgonae
Canis mesomelas schmidti

Red wolf
Canis rufus rufus
Canis rufus gregoryi

Simien jackal
Canis simensis simensis
Canis simensis citernii

Crab-eating zorro
Cerdocyon thous thous
Cerdocyon thous aquilus
Cerdocyon thous azarae
Cerdocyon thous entrerianus
Cerdocyon thous germanus

Maned wolf
Chrysocyon brachyurus

Dhole
Cuon alpinus alpinus
Cuon alpinus adustus
Cuon alpinus dukhunensis
Cuon alpinus fumosus

Dhole (*continued*)
Cuon alpinus hesperius
Cuon alpinus infuscus
Cuon alpinus javanocus
Cuon alpinus laniger
Cuon alpinus lepturus
Cuon alpinus primaevus
Cuon alpinus sumatrensis

Culpeo
Dusicyon culpaeus culpaeus
Dusicyon culpaeus andinus
Dusicyon culpaeus culpaeolus
Dusicyon culpaeus lycoides
Dusicyon culpaeus magellanicus
Dusicyon culpaeus reissii
Dusicyon culpaeus smithersi

Grey zorro
Dusicyon griseus griseus
Dusicyon griseus domeykoanus
Dusicyon griseus fulvipes
Dusicyon griseus gracilis
Dusicyon griseus maullinicus

Azara's zorro
Dusicyon gymnocercus gymnocercus
Dusicyon gymnocercus antiquus
Dusicyon gymnocercus inca

Sechuran zorro
Dusicyon sechurae

Hoary zorro
Dusicyon vetulus

Small-eared zorro
Dusicyon microtis

Fennec fox
Fennecus zerda

African wild dog
Lycaon pictus pictus
Lycaon pictus lupinus
Lycaon pictus manguensis
Lycaon pictus sharicus
Lycaon pictus somalicus

Raccoon dog
Nyctereutes procyonoides procyonoides
Nyctereutes procyonoides koreensis
Nyctereutes procyonoides orestes
Nyctereutes procyonoides ussuriensis
Nyctereutes procyonoides viverrinus

Bat-eared fox
Otocyon megalotis megalotis
Octocyon megalotis virgatus

Bush dog
Speothos venaticus venaticus
Speothos venaticus wingei

Grey fox
Urocyon cinereoargenteus cinereoargenteus
Urocyon cinereoargenteus borealis
Urocyon cinereoargenteus californicus
Urocyon cinereoargenteus colimensis
Urocyon cinereoargenteus costaricensis
Urocyon cinereoargenteus floridanus
Urocyon cinereoargenteus fraterculus
Urocyon cinereoargenteus furvus
Urocyon cinereoargenteus guatemalae
Urocyon cinereoargenteus madrensis
Urocyon cinereoargenteus nigrirostris
Urocyon cinereoargenteus ocythous
Urocyon cinereoargenteus orinomus
Urocyon cinereoargenteus peninsularis
Urocyon cinereoargenteus scottii
Urocyon cinereoargenteus townsendi
Urocyon cinereoargenteus venezuelae

Island grey fox
Urocyon littoralis littoralis
Urocyon littoralis catalinae
Urocyon littoralis clementae
Urocyon littoralis dickeyi
Urocyon littoralis santacruzae
Urocyon littoralis santarosae

Bengal fox
Vulpes bengalensis

Blanford's fox
Vulpes cana

Cape fox
Vulpes chama

Corsac fox
Vulpes corsac corsac
Vulpes corsac kalmykorum
Vulpes corsac turkmenica

Tibetan fox
Vulpes ferrilata

Pale fox
Vulpes pallida pallida
Vulpes pallida edwardsi
Vulpes pallida harterti
Vulpes pallida oertzeni

Rüppell's fox
Vulpes rueppelli rueppelli
Vulpes rueppelli caesia
Vulpes rueppelli cufrana
Vulpes rueppelli somaliae

Swift fox
Vulpes velox velox
Vulpes velox arsipus
Vulpes velox devia
Vulpes velox hebes
Vulpes velox macrotis
Vulpes velox mutica
Vulpes velox neomexicana
Vulpes velox nevadensis
Vulpes velox tenuirostris
Vulpes velox zinseri

Red fox
Vulpes vulpes vulpes
Vulpes vulpes abietorum
Vulpes vulpes aeygptiaca
Vulpes vulpes alascensis
Vulpes vulpes alpherakyi
Vulpes vulpes alticola
Vulpes vulpes anatolica
Vulpes vulpes arabica
Vulpes vulpes atlantica
Vulpes vulpes barbaras
Vulpes vulpes beringiana
Vulpes vulpes cascadensis
Vulpes vulpes caucasica

Red fox (*continued*)
Vulpes vulpes crucigera
Vulpes vulpes daurica
Vulpes vulpes diluta
Vulpes vulpes dolichocrania
Vulpes vulpes dorsalis
Vulpes vulpes flavescens
Vulpes vulpes fulva
Vulpes vulpes griffithi
Vulpes vulpes harrimani
Vulpes vulpes hoole
Vulpes vulpes ichnusae
Vulpes vulpes induta
Vulpes vulpes jakutensis
Vulpes vulpes japonica
Vulpes vulpes karagan
Vulpes vulpes kenaiensis

Vulpes vulpes krimeamontana
Vulpes vulpes kurdistanica
Vulpes vulpes macroura
Vulpes vulpes montana
Vulpes vulpes necator
Vulpes vulpes ochroxantha
Vulpes vulpes palaestina
Vulpes vulpes peculiosa
Vulpes vulpes pusilla
Vulpes vulpes regalis
Vulpes vulpes rubricosa
Vulpes vulpes schrencki
Vulpes vulpes silacea
Vulpes vulpes splendidissima
Vulpes vulpes stepensis
Vulpes vulpes tobolica
Vulpes vulpes tschiliensis

Further Reading

Although a number of titles in this list are out of print, they should be available from a specialist natural history book dealer, or possibly from a public library.

Alderton, David (1984), *The Dog*, Macdonald, London.
Alderton, David (1993), *Eyewitness Handbook: Dogs*, Dorling Kindersley, London.
Bedi, Ramesh and Rajesh (1984), *Indian Wildlife*, Collins, London.
Brown, D. E., ed. (1983), *The Wolf in the Southwest*, Arizona University Press, Arizona.
Bueler, Lois E. (1974), *Wild Dogs of the World*, Constable, London.
Burbank, James C. (1990), *Vanishing Lobo: The Mexican Wolf and the Southwest*, Johnson Books, Boulder.
Burrows, Roger (1968), *Wild Fox: A Complete Study of the Red Fox*, David & Charles, Newton Abbot.
Burton, John A. and Pearson, Bruce (1987), *Collins Guide to Rare Mammals of the World*, Collins, London.
Chalanae, Victor, H. (1947), *Mammals of North America*, Macmillan, New York.
Clutton-Brook, Juliet (1987), *A Natural History of Domesticated Animals*, Cambridge University Press, Cambridge.
Copper, Basil (1977), *The Werewolf in Legend, Fact and Art*, Robert Hale, London.
Day, David (1981), *The Domesday Book of Animals*, Ebury Press, London.
Delibes, Miguel (1990), *Status and Conservation Needs of the Wolf (Canis lupus) in the Council of Europe Member States*, Nature & Environment Series no. 47, Council of Europe, Strasbourg.
Ewer, R. T. (1973), *The Carnivores*, Weidenfeld & Nicolson, London.
Fiennes, Richard and Alice (1968), *The Natural History of the Dog*, Weidenfeld & Nicolson, London.
Fox, Michael W., ed. (1983), *The Wild Canids: Their Systematics, Behavioral Ecology and Evolution*, Krieger, Florida.
Fox, Michael W. (1984), *The Whistling Hunters: Field Studies of the Asiatic Wild Dog (Cuon alpinus)*, SUNY, Albany, New York.
Fox, Michael W. (1987), *Behavior of Wolves, Dogs and Related Canids*, Krieger, Florida.
Ginsberg, J. R. and Macdonald, D. W. (1990), *Foxes, Wolves, Jackals, and Dogs: An Action Plan for the Conservation of Canids*, IUCN, Gland, Switzerland.
Grzimek, H. C. (1984), *Grzimek's Animal Life Encyclopedia*, Vol. 12, Van Nostrand Reinhold, New York.
Grzimek, H. C. (1990), *Grzimek's Encyclopedia: Mammals*, Vol. 4, McGraw-Hill, New York.

Halstead, L. B. (1978), *The Evolution of Mammals*, Peter Lowe, London.

Haltenorth, Theodor and Diller, Helmut (1980), *A Field Guide to the Mammals of Africa including Madagascar*, Collins, London.

Jackson, Peter and Sheean-Stone, Olga (1991), *Wild Dogs and their Relatives*, IUCN, Gland, Switzerland.

Kingdom, J. (1977), *East African Mammals*, Vol. 3A, Academic Press, London.

Kurten, Bjorn (1971), *The Age of Mammals*, Weidenfeld & Nicolson, London.

Leopold, Aldo S. (1959), *Wildlife of Mexico*, University of California Press, Berkeley.

Leydet, Francois (1988), *The Coyote: Defiant Songdog of the West*, University of Oklahoma, Norman.

Lever, Sir Christopher (1985), *Naturalized Mammals of the World*, Longman, London.

Macdonald, David, ed. (1984), *The Encyclopedia of Mammals*, Vol. 1, George Allen & Unwin, London.

Macdonald, David (1992), *The Velvet Claw: A Natural History of the Carnivores*, BBC Books, London.

McFarland, David, ed. (1987), *The Oxford Companion to Animal Behaviour*, Oxford University Press, Oxford.

Matthews, L. Harrison (1969), *The Life of Mammals*, Vols 1 and 2, Weidenfeld & Nicolson, London.

Mech, L. David (1981), *The Wolf: The Ecology and Behavior of an Endangered Species*, University of Minnesota, Minneapolis.

Mech, L. David (1992), *The Way of the Wolf*, Swan Hill Press, Shropshire.

Novak, Ronald M. and Paradiso, John L. (1983), *Walker's Mammals of the World*, Vols 1 and 2, Johns Hopkins University Press, Baltimore.

St. George, E. A. (1987), *A Guide to the Gods of Ancient Egypt*, Spock Press, London.

Savage, R. J. G. and Long, M. R. (1986), *Mammal Evolution – An Illustrated Guide*, Facts on File, New York.

Sheldon, Jennifer W. (1992), *Wild Dogs: The Natural History of the Nondomestic Canidae*, Academic Press, San Diego.

Stuttard, R. M., ed. (1986), *Predatory Mammals in Britain*, The British Field Sports Society/RSNC/FFPS/The Game Conservancy/The Gamekeepers' Association, London.

Whitfield, Philip (1978), *The Hunters*, Hamlyn, London.

Young, Stanley P. and Jackson, Hartley H. T. (1978), *The Clever Coyote*, Bison Books, University of Nebraska Press, Lincoln.

Zimen, Erik (1978), *The Wolf: His Place in the Natural World*, Souvenir Press, London.

Index

Page numbers in *italic* refer to black and white illustrations. Page numbers in **bold** refer to colour plates. Specific information can be found also under individual species' entries.